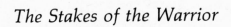

The Stakes of the Warrior

The Stakes of the Warrior

Georges Dumézil

Translated by David Weeks
Edited, with an Introduction,
by Jaan Puhvel

UNIVERSITY OF CALIFORNIA PRESS
Berkeley Los Angeles London

University of California Press
Berkeley and Los Angeles, California

University of California Press, Ltd.
London, England

Library of Congress Cataloging in Publication Data

Dumézil, Georges, 1898–
The stakes of the warrior.

Translation of: L'enjeu du jeu des dieux—un héros (which is pt. 1 of v. 2, Types epipues indo-européens—un héros, un sorcier, un roi, of Mythe et épopée)
1. Mythology, Indo-European. I. Puhvel, Jaan.
II. Title.
BL660.D793513 1983 291.1'3'809034 82-13384
ISBN 0-520-04834-2

Printed in the United States of America

1 2 3 4 5 6 7 8 9

Contents

Editor's Preface

Georges Dumézil's three-volume opus *Mythe et épopée* (1968, 1971, 1973) has become, for better or worse, a kind of quarry, subject to piecemeal extractions into the English language. A start was made with *The Destiny of a King* (University of Chicago Press, 1973), covering the last third of *ME II*. Subsequently the bulk of *ME III* has been made available as *Camillus* by the University of California Press (1980). The editor of the latter, Udo Strutynski, anticipated the present undertaking by formulating a desideratum as follows (p. 261): ". . . surely the next order of business should be to make Dumézil's latest—and presumably final—word on the warrior complex available by bringing out a translation of the first part of *Mythe et épopée II*. . . . This theoretical disquisition on the heroic predicament constitutes a tightly knit monograph in its own right as it takes the argument begun in *Destiny of the Warrior* through uncharted waters and launches a new perspective on the problem. It is self-evident that without a full understanding of the tensions and contrasts at work between the earlier and later studies no further progress on the warrior question can occur."

With the presentation below of "L'enjeu du jeu des dieux: un héros," introduced by a critical essay, all but the central third of *ME II* (concerning the Indic sorcerer Kāvya Uśanas, of Indo-Iranian rather than Indo-European relevance) is now available in vernacular to what the French are wont to call "le monde anglo-saxon." This leaves in the main only the monumental first volume, Dumézil's summa on the *Mahābhārata*, Roman "history," the Ossetic epic, and "epica minora," as a future agendum.

For most quotations from Saxo Grammaticus the new English translation by Peter Fisher (1979) is used in preference to Oliver Elton's old version, except that the Latin forms of proper names have been retained. The renderings of certain of Saxo's quoted Latin poems, however, as well as all quoted passages from Old Icelandic, are of the translator's and editor's making and based directly on the original.

For the *Mahābhārata* Dumézil uses interchangeably the Calcutta and Poona editions. Whenever the latter occurs in extensive quotations, the English version given is normally that of J. A. B. van Buitenen's Chicago translation (1973–); where the two editions run parallel, with no or insignificant variations, van Buitenen's rendering (with occasional slight corrections) also serves for Dumézil's use of the Calcutta edition; but in cases of significant divergence or inaccuracy, the Calcutta passages are translated directly from the Sanskrit, and the same is true in glossing all short snatches of Sanskrit in the running text.

Quoted passages from Diodorus Siculus are given in the translation of C. H. Oldfather (Loeb Classical Library, 1935), with some changes in the spelling of proper names.

Of the appendices to *ME II*, only the extracts from de Polier's *Mythologie des Indous* which relate to Jarāsandha and Śiśupāla (pp. 381–388) have been included; appendix II (pp. 392–402, text and French translation of Saxo's seventy Sapphic stanzas containing Starcatherus's torrent of invective against Ingellus) is unnecessary in English, given the available renderings by both Elton and Fisher.

Editor's Introduction

With *Aspects de la fonction guerrière chez les Indo-européens* (1956; German edition 1964) and its revamped version *Heur et malheur du guerrier* = *The Destiny of the Warrior* (1970), Georges Dumézil inaugurated a systematic investigation of the Indo-European warrior type by matching the Roman "epic" of Tullus Hostilius with Vedic myths surrounding Indra, more specifically the combined "third vs. triple" and killing-of-kin themes (Horatii vs. Curiatii, Trita Āptya vs. Triśiras) and the episode of the treacherous ally (Namuci, Mettius) over whom the hero prevails with the aid of succorous deities (Sarasvatī-Aśvins, Quirinus-Ops) and whom he slays in the end by cruel and unusual, thus "sinful" means. Dumézil also stressed the "solitude and liberty" characteristics of the Indo-European warrior, as exemplified by Indra's epithet *éka-*, 'one, alone, unique,' his avyayībhāva adverb *yathā-vaśám*, 'as one wills,' and his noun *svadhā́*, 'one's own law, autonomy.' The latter's cognate relationship with Latin *sodālis*, 'member of a secret society,' pointed up the warrior's ambivalent role as single champion or part of a self-centered corps or coterie, both a society's external defender and its potential internal menace.

As symptomatic of such a mythic warrior's "life story" Dumézil singled out "negative peaks" or perhaps nadir-episodes, a structured set of misdeeds or failings in which the hero compromises his career by offending all three levels of society by murderous/ sacrilegious, cowardly/ unwarriorlike, and venal/ adulterous acts respectively. Thus Indra, spared censure in Vedic hymns for the simple reason that one does not dwell on the seamy side of one's object of celebration, has his antisocial proclivities fully aired in Brāhmaṇic, Epic, and Purāṇic texts, especially Book Five of the *Mārkaṇḍeya-Purāṇa* where Indra's killing of his fellow god Tvaṣṭar's son Triśiras and of Vṛtra (replacing Namuci), and sexual possession of Ahalyā in the disguise of her husband Gautama, cause him to be divested of his splendor, might, and looks (*tejas, balam, rūpam*) which are transferred to Dharma, Māruta (= Vāyu), and the Nāsatya (= Aśvin) twins respectively (and subsequently deposited in the wombs of the queens Kuntī and Mādrī, engendering the Mahābhārata heroes Yudhiṣṭhira, Bhīma + Arjuna, and Nakula + Sahadeva). Dumézil saw a parallel in the Avestan "first king" and culture hero Yima who when sinning lost his regal glory (*x^{v}arənah*) in staggered portions which were successively reinvested in Mithra, Thraetaona, and Kṛsāspa. Three similar low points in the sagas of Starcatherus in Saxo Grammaticus (regicidal human sacrifice inspired by Odin, uncharacteristic cowardice in battle, "contract" killing for gold of a king in his bath) and of Herakles in Diodorus Siculus (defiance of Zeus leading to madness resulting in the killing of his own children in rage brought on by Hera, ruseful defenestration of Iphitus, adultery with Iole) supplied Germanic and Greek reinforcements of the typology.

This work, attractively presented, closely reasoned, and full of intriguing parallelisms, received further substantiation in *Mythe et épopée* II (1971) and III (1973). The hero as the stakes in a game of gods—such is the title Dumézil bestowed on his treatment of the "parallel lives" of Starcatherus, Śiśupāla, and Herakles in *ME II*, pp. 13–132 = the present book, a work which makes the earlier study seem a superficial sketch. Yima and Indra have been excluded from the dossier, the former without explanation *in loco*. In *Heur et malheur* pp. 94–95 = *Destiny of the Warrior* pp. 103–104 Yima's non-warrior status was explained via the doctrinal "demilitarization" of the Zoroastrian reform, whereas now (*ME II*, pp. 356–

358 = *The Destiny of a King* pp. 110–112 [1973]) Yima stands apart altogether, charged rather with a single (albeit triply compartmentalized), all-encompassing "sin of the sovereign" radically different in kind from the "three sins of the warrior." Indra's eviction is explicit: The *Mārkaṇḍeya-Purāṇa* account is pronounced a secondary, artificial mythological extension of the epic theme of the three sins (see below, pp. 4–5, 140) which latter Dumézil finds rather tucked away in the figures of Śiśupāla + Jarāsandha in the *Mahābhārata*. These refinements started from a realization that peculiar concordances of the mortal careers of Starcatherus and Herakles, from the setting of their fates by antagonistic deities of the "first two functions" (Odin–Thor, Hera–Athena) to their quasi-self-immolational death using the services of a young assistant (Hatherus, Philoktetes), outweigh the single theme of the three sins.

The resulting study of three heroic careers attains important new levels of penetration in the Starcatherus part, giving their due also to Old Icelandic sources for Starkaðr (especially the *Gautreks-saga*). It also analyzes in depth for the first time the strange figures of Śiśupāla and his supplementary analogue and overking Jarāsandha. The Herakles part, however, remains as before somewhat sketchy and inconclusive. Dumézil nevertheless triangulates the Scandinavian, Indic, and Greek traditions and reaches the startling conclusion that the Scandinavian–Greek isotheme bundle constitutes the strongest axis, with the Scandinavian–Indic one a clear second, and the Greek–Indic one an almost nonexistent third. Thus the Starcatherus story, despite its late attestation, is the common denominator and hence the purest reflector of Indo-European inheritance. Rather than a triangle, the whole is triptych, with Scandinavia as centerpiece and India and Greece as side panels.

Some of the discrepancies and "loose ends" in the Herakles saga are readily explicable as culturally conditioned innovations. Unlike Starcatherus and Śiśupāla with their innate enormities (supernumerary arms [+ eye in Śiśupāla]) which are corrected in childhood by divine intervention, Herakles is "normal" for the simple reason that he conforms to the Greek norm which eschews congenital monstrosity in Olympian heroes, reserving hand-related and ocular irregularities for the former gods of the Titan generation (Hekatonkheiroi, Kyklopes). Rather than undergo decapitation in the manner of Starcatherus or Śiśupāla, Herakles has a mysterious apotheosis by fire on a mountain, in conformity with the classical heroic pattern. In contradistinction to the ultra-royalists Starcatherus and Śiśupāla who nevertheless become regicidally entangled (counting Jarāsandha as alter ego of Śiśupāla), Herakles has no similar extreme proclivities; apart from his strained service to Eurystheus, his legend conforms to the relative obsoleteness of human sacrifice (or at least the immolation of kings) in classical Greece, unlike the persistence of ritualistic murder in pagan Scandinavia and its vestigial reminiscences in both Vedic legend and ritual and in the laws of Manu.

But interest centers on the "game of gods" in which the hero is the "stakes" (perhaps one might call him rather the pawn in a divine tug-of-war), and here, too, Herakles is notably discrepant. Unlike Starcatherus buffeted in the tension-field between Odin and Thor, and Śiśupāla, human replica of Rudra-Śiva, face to face with Kṛṣṇa, an avatar of Viṣṇu, Herakles is the victim/beneficiary of the attentions of two female deities, Hera and Athena. This feature, too, can be explained as a Greek innovation, attributable to the role that the Olympian offshoots of the Aegean goddesses typically play in the careers of individual heroes (e. g., Athena with Odysseus); Zeus is in such cases above the fray, or in this instance working for his son through the proxy of his head-born daughter, with Olympian household tensions replacing inherited Indo-European antagonisms.

Since Indo-European structures are involved in this epic plot, neither sectarian oppositions between Odin-cult and Thor-worship in Viking Scandinavia, nor the Vaiṣṇava/Śaiva split of Hinduism, nor the absence of any such historical schism in the Olympian system are of relevance (the Olympian : chthonian dichotomy does not enter). Dumézil is naturally prone to applying the trifunctional analysis and to extrapolating from such typecasting. Thus Odin is essentially of the "first function," Thor "second function," as are Hera and Athena respectively, chiefly on the basis of the anecdotal Judgment of Paris, while Rudra and Viṣṇu are not "functionally integrated" (still, Vasus, Rudras, and Ādityas sum up the formulaic roster of the tripartite pantheon [*RV* 10.128.9], and Rudr[iy]as = Maruts are clearly warrior deities). Dumézil is of course aware of the functional shifts and slippages in Germanic theology, with Odin's warlike preoccupations and Thor's impingements on the rain-related concerns of the husbandmen. He is also quite willing to admit further complexity in Odin, latching on to the comparisons made by Jan de Vries and others between Odin and Rudra. Thus a different, extrafunctional opposition of "dark" (Odin, Rudra) and "light" (Thor, Viṣṇu) deities is set up, one that is more serious for the tripartite system than was Dumézil's one-time distinction of "first" and "last" gods, since it cuts across such stalwarts of trifunctionality as Odin and Thor. Dumézil realizes that this "dark" : "light" opposition lies at the heart of the antagonisms that victimize the hero, and yet he is unable to find any trace of it in Hera : Athena, leaving this ἀπορία for others to solve (see below, p. 132).

For further understanding of this saga we might expunge all reference to the "first function" and treat it as purely internal to the warrior class, with the "dark" : "light" opposition basic to the inner tensions of that class. Such distinctions as the "chivalrous" vs. "brute" warrior (Indra vs. Vāyu, Arjuna vs. Bhīma, Achilles vs. Herakles; cf. e.g., *Destiny of the Warrior* xi) should likewise be deemphasized as superficial: Thor is called "a kind of Vāyu or Bhīma" (i.e., a "solitary" champion; see below, p. 86), and yet Vāyu's alleged pre-Vedic "brute warrior" character had supposedly turned into that of a "first" (or "initial") god by Vedic times (*Destiny of the Warrior*, p. 59). In short, we should clear the boards also of that non-basic differentation.

For "dark" and "light" I would rather substitute a "demonic" vs. "culture god" opposition between deities of the warrior class. It is the difference between a figure of monstrous ancestry or attachments and one who makes the world safe against monsters, a kind of nature : culture tension in which the warrior is caught up. Rudra with his three eyes and four arms, one-eyed Odin born of the giantess Bestla and riding an eight-legged horse, Hera born of Titans, with one-eyed Kyklopes and hundred-armed Hekatonkheiroi for uncles and herself the parthenogenous mother of the monster Typhoeus—all these fit the "demonic" slot. The hero has definite onomastic associations with this kind of deity: Śiśupāla echoing (Rudra) Paśupati, Starcatherus-Starkaðr being a compound of Hatherus-Höðr (name of both the hero's young deliverer from life and the fate-god himself, close to Odin), and Herakles meaning "possessing Hera's κλέος." The contrasting deity is one who prunes the wild by holding down the monstrous (Indra or Trita Āptya slaying Triśiras, Thor cutting back on giants, Athena Nike with the Gorgon's head on her breastplate) and furthering normal nature (Indra and Thor releasing waters, Trita Āptya being "watery" in his very clan-name, Athena nurturing both plants [olive] and the young [Erikhthonios]). Vāyu may well originally belong on the "wild" side, and Indra has become too much of an all-round warrior god to admit full and sharp polarization; but Viṣṇu is a good candidate for the "culture god" type, not only in his Kṛṣṇa-avatar but also in that of Rāma, who after all married the Furrow, Sītā, and whose story is homologous to the Indra-myths of the Veda, as Hermann Jacobi showed almost a century ago. Viṣṇu's Norse parallel, Viðar, is typically a strong-arm/foot god second only to Thor himself, one who will not desist from monster-extermination even in the last straits of eschatology, as he forces apart and shatters the jaws of the wolf Fenrir who has devoured Odin. The warrior hero is thus somehow genetically and inherently demonic, and his career is marked by the drama between this ancestral burden and the rehabilitational and "civilizing" efforts under the figurative (and in one case literal) aegis of the opposing deity. Thor performs on Starkaðr a rough form of plastic surgery, Kṛṣṇa relies on more miraculous instant normalization of the infant Śiśupāla, Athena's services to Herakles range from nurture to armament. In line with European heroic tradition, the Norse and Greek strongmen even acquire the finer skills of poetry and music, whereas India lays more stress on the purely demonic. Herakles shows traits reminiscent of the Thor type, perhaps preserving some of the features that have been otherwise lost due to Athena's female gender, such as active monster-killing and the episodes of transvestitism which also characterize Thor and Achilles. In the fullness of time, the god Odin who ordained Starkaðr's three life-spans takes him back unto himself by the offices of Höðr; Zeus arranges for Hera to "adopt" formally the deified Herakles on whose begetting he had spent three symbolic night-spans. Śiśupāla's end comes instead at the hands of Kṛṣṇa, upon which he is absorbed into the godhead of his killer by a Viṣṇuite salvation miracle; this thematic reversal is as understandable in classical India as is the reclaiming of the hero by Odin in Viking Scandinavia; both accounts are simply true to their sectarian environments. The hero's career is in all instances tragic, due to the flaws inherent in his demonic nature or inflicted by the gods vying for his soul, but the resolutions differ: reconciliation in Europe, redemption in India.

Ancillary matter to this great tableau has been accumulating during the 1970s. Akin to the "three sins" is the theme of the "three charges against the warrior," as when the Romans Camillus (μισόδημος according to Plutarch, like the populace-hating Starcatherus) and Coriolanus are accused of sacrilege/usurpation, irregularities in the disposal of military spoils, and opposition to populist measures (*ME* III, pp. 231–235, pp. 242–248). Dumézil himself has compared with the three sins the excessive revenge that the Ossetic hero Batraz exacts for the murder of his father Xaemyc, with successive cruelties against the Boratae (third-estate clan), the Æxsaertaegkatae (warrior estate), and the heavenly powers themselves (angels, spirits), until his death reconciles him to God (*Romans de Scythie et d'alentour* [1978], pp. 50–58). Daniel Dubuisson (*Annales Économies Sociétés Civilisations* 34 [1979], 464–489) has tabulated what he considers the "three sins of Rāma" (unethical slaying of Vālin, brahmanicidal killing of Rāvaṇa, repudiation of Sītā), thereby to a degree affirming Jacobi's thesis of the Indraic sources of the characters and plot of the *Rāmāyaṇa*. Perhaps most interesting of all, David J. Cohen (*Celtica* 12.113–124 [1977]) has challenged Dumézil's claim (see below, p. 141) that "of the numerous great warriors of Irish sagas, none is the subject of a tale which even remotely recalls those that have been studied" (viz. Starkaðr, Śiśupāla, Herakles). Suibhne Geilt in the *Buile Suibhne* is an Irish warrior whose life of wandering and poetry is dramatically highlighted by his unprovoked outrages against St. Rónán, his strange cowardly flight from the battle of Magh Rath, and his violent death in the house of St. Moling on an accusation—albeit false—of adultery, accompanied by last rites administered by St. Moling who had long anticipated Suibhne's coming and was thus fatally foreordained to attend to the final stages of his life. Here Rónán, the church-builder and "constructive" figure in association with kings, clearly occupies the "culture god" slot, and Suibhne's frenetic hatred of him has much in common with Śiśupāla's onslaught on Kṛṣṇa. Moling, on the other hand, figures as the ingatherer of the spent soul of this Sweeney Agonistes in the manner in which Odin arranges for the return of his own: reconciliation of the poet-warrior to his god rather than miraculous transfusional salvation, in line with Scandinavia and Greece rather than India. Cohen also finds an inverted variant of the theme of the "three sins" in the *Bórama Laigen*, which details St. Columb's description of three Irish kings who had gone to heaven, namely, Daimin Damargait who never hassled the church, Ailill who in the nick of time had thought better of fleeing from battle, and Feradach who was beguiled by gold until he repented of his hoarding on his deathbed and at last sought divine grace. Here the pitfalls which the first two "saved" rulers avoided match the first two sins of Suibhne, whereas Feradach's last-minute immunity to *auri sacra fames* looks rather like the antidote that might have saved Starcatherus from his third sin, the mercenary murder of King Olo in return for gold.

Thanks to Dumézil we are on the tracks of a truly Indo-European hero-typology, one that mirrors an epic myth once current in traditions from Iceland and Ireland to Iran and India, greatly at variance with the ritualistic and psychoanalytic prototypes postulated for the "average" hero figure by the likes of Lord Raglan, Otto Rank, and Joseph Campbell.

Introduction

The work presented here follows up a study made in a course at the Collège de France in March 1953, published in 1956 in *Aspects de la fonction guerrière*, and reproduced with few alterations in 1970 in *The Destiny of the Warrior*, pp. 51–107.

It was in 1953 that three examples were assembled of a remarkable epic thematization of the Indo-European trifunctional structure which I proposed to call, for short, "the three sins of the warrior." They concern an Indic god, Indra, a Scandinavian hero, Starkaðr (Starcatherus), and a Greek hero, Herakles. The theme provides the two heroes with the general outline of their careers, from youth to death, while it accounts for only a segment of the god's career, one leading to a temporary but nearly complete downfall.

According to the fifth section of the *Mārkaṇḍeya-Purāṇa*, in an act which is necessary for the well-being of the world but inherently censurable, Indra kills a demonic being who holds the rank of Brahman and who is according to some also the priest of the gods and even their kinsman; this sacrilegious act causes the murderer to lose his *tejas*, his spiritual energy. Later he treacherously slays a second demon of whom he, the warrior, has been afraid and whom, contrary to his calling, he has not dared to confront in a fair fight; as a result of this cowardice he loses his *bala*, his physical strength. Finally, like Jupiter with Amphitryon, he dons the appearance of a husband whose wife he covets and thus gets his way; this sexual villainy makes him lose his *rūpa*, his beauty. Nothing remains to him except, since this immortal naturally must live on, a small portion of the *bala*, the strength which is the essence of his own function. Consequently he is virtually wiped out, and his situation is the more serious as the *tejas*, the *bala*, and the *rūpa* that have deserted him seem irrecoverable, each having entered into the god with whom it has a natural affinity: his spiritual energy has flowed into Dharma, the personification of right as well as morality; his physical strength into Vāyu, the brutish Wind; his beauty into the two handsome divine twins, the Aśvins. These four gods, plus what remains of Indra himself, later beget on Pāṇḍu's behalf an equal number of sons, who finally make up the famous trifunctional group of the five Pāṇḍava brothers (or half brothers, or near brothers).

In the summation by Diodorus Siculus, the long string of Herakles' feats, so helpful to men and to the gods, is set off, punctuated by three failings whose effects are serious and which necessitate, besides a consultation of the priestess of Delphi, some expiation or redress. For having tried to avoid the divine command which sent him into the service of Eurystheus, he is seized with madness (λύσσα), kills his children, and overcome by this deed, must resign himself to perform the labors which Eurystheus dreams up, with a number of sub-labors. With this task done, he kills, by a shameful trick and not in a fair fight, an enemy who is next to him; he is then stricken with a physical illness (νοσήσας) which he can be rid of only by becoming, on the advice of the Pythia, the slave of Omphale, queen of Lydia. Finally, after a new series of "free" deeds, he forgets that he has just formally and legally married Deianeira and enters into a culpable relationship, as the direct consequence of which he is bodily devoured by the burning (θερμασία) of the tunic soaked in the blood of Nessos, and after a last consultation with the Pythia ascends the pyre of Oeta.

In the treatment of Saxo Grammaticus, the only complete one, the no less lengthy and varied string of exploits of the hero Starcatherus is spread out over three periods, more precisely three lives, each of which is of necessity and by preordination marked by a *facinus*, a felony. He helps the god Othinus kill a Norwegian king, his master and friend, in a simulated human sacrifice. After the death of another master, a Swedish king, he flees shamefully from the battlefield, contributing to the rout of the army. Finally, he lets himself be bribed by conspirators, for a hundred and twenty pounds of gold, and kills a third master, the Danish king Olo.

Brahmanicide, cowardice instead of valor, base adultery; such is the criminal record of Indra. Disobedience to Zeus, cowardice instead of bravery, and neglect of conjugal duty constitute the dossier of Herakles. And that of Starcatherus includes murder of his king in a human sacrifice, flight on the battlefield after the death of his king, and murder of his king for cash money. Each of these three sets violates in succession the laws of religion, the warrior's ethic, and one or the other of the two most important components—sexuality and wealth—of the morality of the third function.

This parallelism was certainly no illusion, but what lesson did it offer? Since 1953 I had singled out among the three documents, taken in pairs, further binary accordances in which the third did not share. Thus only the sins of Indra and of Herakles, for which the culprits are fully responsible, entail separate, immediate, automatic sanctions, while those of Starcatherus, the results of a curse against which he is powerless, have no such effects. Yet even here the similarity involves an important difference: while Indra loses successively, without intervening restoration, the three components of his being (spiritual energy, physical strength, beauty), thus heading continuously and linearly towards his temporary downfall after the third sin and the third loss, on the contrary the "madness," then the "sickness" of Herakles are completely cured, each after an atonement; his mental and physical health are restored, and it is the third sin alone which puts him in a state for which there is no other remedy than a voluntary death. By the same token, the Greek structure is closer to the Scandinavian in which the first two *facinora* have no ill effects, but where Starcatherus, once the third is committed, has but one idea, one need: to offer himself willingly to the sword of a killer chosen by himself. In short, the width of the divergences imposed the view—hence the title given to the 1956 essay—that only the general framework of the "three sins of the warrior" is to be ascribed to Indo-European inheritance, and that each of the three societies has made use of it independently and in an original manner.

And yet, between Starkaðr-Starcatherus and Herakles, besides this general outline, there appeared very specific correspondences: not only their voluntary death, but their type of champion, as righters of wrongs wandering throughout the world; the paid help which they seek and get from a young friend for the sort of death which they have chosen; and above all, in their beginnings, the two antagonistic divinities who set or enjoin their fates, and who turn out to be those of the first two functions on well-known canonical lists: Odin and Thor, Hera and Athena. Thus one could glimpse the main features of a common plot, where the three sins were merely one correspondence among others. But how was one to interpret this broad agreement in which India did not share?

Actually, the comparative dossier was somewhat unbalanced, by the simple fact that it entailed two human heroes in contrast with a god: Indra's sins are mythological, those of Starkaðr and of Herakles are epic. This of course does not preclude comparison, but there was a more troublesome problem. Critics have not failed to note that the Indic document used was a Purāṇa, the valuable *Mārkaṇḍeya-Purāṇa* to be sure, which has preserved other certainly archaic material, but which one would like to back up here with an epic version; as matters stand, although a text of the *Mahābhārata* does expound a theory of the downfall of Indra in the same sense, it lacks precisely what would be important, the theme of the three sins. Thus one cannot exclude the possibility that a relatively late author had systematized the sins, or at least some of the sins of Indra—a well-known notion ever since Vedic prose literature, as is moreover the theme of the god's "losses"—within the frame of the three functions which was suggested to him by the end of the story, the begetting of the Pāṇḍavas by the gods of these functions.

More generally, the idea that a warrior, man or god, successively commits a spectacular sin in each of the three areas (social, moral, even cosmic) defined by the three functions, is not so unique that it could not have been reinvented independently in several places, in several societies where the ideology of the three functions remained alive and dominant. It is all a matter of context. But in fact, the context of the "sins of Indra" in the *Mārkaṇḍeya-Purāṇa* is entirely different from that of the sins of Starkaðr and Herakles. The third term of the comparison being thus weakened, and perhaps secondary, there remained face to face only the saga and Diodorus—with the margin of indeterminacy inherent in any comparative study where the dossier has been reduced to two witnesses.

Another section of the 1953 study also required additional investigation. With regard to Starkaðr, it had seemed natural and easy, going beyond the theme of the three sins, to interpret his career as a whole, and to do so by relying on Saxo Grammaticus: does not he alone present entire, in all its three parts and with great clarity, the panorama of *facinora* which are merely mentioned by Old Icelandic texts? I therefore preferred Saxo's account for other points of the saga where it does not agree with the Icelandic sources, and in particular for a most important point, since it is one of those where, in addition to the theme of the three sins, the legend of Herakles and that of Starkaðr manifest a specific accordance: the relationships of the hero with two divinities who are variously interested in him, Hera and Athena, Odin and Thor. Consequently, I categorized Starkaðr as a "hero of Thor," a rare specimen in contrast to the abundantly attested "Odinic hero." Thor, in fact, seems in Saxo's account to be completely benevolent towards Starcatherus, since his only, but decisive, intercession is to rectify the hero's monstrous birth and give him a human form which is indispensable for his prestigious career, whereas Othinus, besides unarguable benefits, is wholly responsible for the imposed fate which sullies this career by three crimes.

This interpretation has encountered more opposition than assent, and constructive critics, such as my late friend Jan de Vries and Mr. Edward O. G. Turville Petre, have objected that the oldest datum, the allusion made by a ninth-century skald to an apparently contemporary tradition, can be understood only if one admits, in agreement with the *Gautrekssaga* and against Saxo, that Thor had well and truly killed a giant named Starkaðr, who can only be, as the saga calls him, a "first Starkaðr," the hero's grandfather.

Thus it was necessary to revise so debatable a solution, which was, however, reinforced by the case of Herakles; persecuted by Hera, protected by Athena, in a context where these two goddesses are in fact, differentially, the Sovereign and the Warrioress, is not the Greek hero the brother of this Starcatherus whom the magical sovereign Othinus favors only to gain his first crime, and to whom the champion Thor first gave human form while leaving him the strength of a giant?

The study of the "three sins of the warrior" thus remained for nearly a decade burdened with a double uncertainty: both as to the value of the Indic data, and as to the meaning to be given to the fate of the Scandinavian hero and consequently to the obvious similarity of his career to that of Herakles. No new decisive element appeared, and there was no room to pursue debates where no argument on either side could be definitive. As often happens, the solution was found on the trail of another inquiry altogether.

Since 1947, and Stig Wikander's discovery about the mythical basis of the *Mahābhārata*, I had continued to explore its numerous and important consequences, for the interpretation of the poem itself as well as for the comparative use of the very archaic mythology uncovered beneath the epic transposition. Several times the inquiry revealed remarkable correspondences between this para-Vedic, often pre-Vedic, mythology and Scandinavian mythology; thus it is that the Dyauḥ who acts indirectly through Bhīṣma, with his extraordinary birth and his role in the dynasty, matches the Heimdallr-Rígr of the Edda, and that the "eschatological battle" lurking beneath the battle of Kurukṣetra has no closer parallel than Ragnarök. Very soon one character caught my attention, both because he seemed by nature to belong to another period of Indic mythology, and because at the same time he lent himself, especially in his role as savior *in extremis*, to precise comparisons with Scandinavian mythology: namely Kṛṣṇa, and through him Viṣṇu. The essence of what I think I can offer on this subject is found in *Mythe et Épopée I*, in the last chapter of Part One ("Annihilation and Rebirth"), but so vast a problem cannot be exhausted, or even encompassed, in the space of a few years. Kṛṣṇa, more exactly the Kṛṣṇa of the *Mahābhārata*, must be looked at not only in his general role as adviser and protector of the Pāṇḍavas, but in all his individual interventions. His particularly close relationship with Arjuna; the freedom which he, and he alone, has to authorize and suggest questionable actions, even lies, without tarnishment; his participation in a battle in which he nevertheless does not fight; the odd pair which he makes with his brother Balarāma, and many other peculiarities invite some thought and undoubtedly reserve happy surprises for the comparativist. It was at one point in this investigation, already long and yet hardly begun, that Kṛṣṇa provided Starkaðr—and through him Herakles—with the Indic "brother" whose place Indra had filled uncomfortably.

It is in the second book of the *Mahābhārata* that Kṛṣṇa first intervenes significantly in the life of the Pāṇḍavas. He persuades the eldest brother Yudhiṣṭhira, who is apparently reconciled with his obnoxious cousins, the sons of Dhṛtarāṣṭra, to celebrate the sacrifice of royal enthronement which in this context also takes on imperial significance: Yudhiṣṭhira will be not only king in his own realm, but recognized sovereign over all the kings of India. By his advice and by several deeds, Kṛṣṇa actually directs the preparations and the accomplishment of the rites. In particular, he eliminates two (moreover interrelated) obstacles: before the ceremony, a rival king; at the beginning of the ceremony itself, what might be called a contestant. This latter is named Śiśupāla, and his bizarre story is recounted in great detail. This was what we were waiting for.

From 25 January to 15 March 1962, in seven seminars at the Collège de France, I attempted to tame this unmanageable character. Since then the study has progressed, and what follows is an account of its current state.

I

STARKAÐR

1. THE TEXTS

The tale of Starkaðr is preserved in two important documents, one of which is accompanied by a small group of brief and fragmentary records which add nothing consequential to it, but the contents of these two documents are very unequal.

One was composed in Old Icelandic, by an author well-versed in ancient tradition, and preserves, interspersed with the prose, a poem in which the hero himself is supposed to be speaking.[1] Unfortunately the period of life covered by this poem and story is limited, extending only from the birth of Starkaðr until shortly after

[1] The *Gautrekssaga,* chaps. 3–7, is cited in the edition of Wilhelm Ranisch, *Palaestra* XI (1900), 11–34. On this saga, see Jan de Vries, *Altnordische Literaturgeschichte* II (1942), 455–457. The poem, *Víkarsbálkr,* contains thirty two stanzas, which are stanzas 6–37 of the saga; it is found, with critical notes and vocabulary, in Andreas Heusler and Wilhelm Ranisch, *Eddica Minora* (1903), 38–43; *pace* these authors, pp. xxx–xxxi, there is no decisive reason to think that stanzas 16–23 (= saga 21–28) were interpolations. The main connected text is *Hervararsaga ok Heiðreks konungs,* ed. Jón Helgason (1924), I:1–2, with variants unimportant for the story. On the local folklore, or pseudo-folklore, of Starkaðr (tombs, etc.), see the very interesting article by Valter Jansson, "Medelpadssägnerna om Starkotter," *Ångermanland-Medelpad, Årsbok för Västernorrlands Läns Hembygdsförbund* (1935), 57–69; also Arvid Enqvist, "Starkotters grav i Wattjom, Medelpad," *Folkminnen och Folktankar,* XXIX (1942), 1–11; Daniel Åslund, "Tuna Socken," *Det gamla Medelpad* III (1946), 39–41 ("Starkodders saga berättad av en 92-årig båtsman").

his first crime. It was only this period which interested the *sagamaðr*, for whom Starkaðr was no more than an accessory figure in a book whose subject was quite different. In fact he is presented to us, at the beginning of the "long version" of the *Gautrekssaga*, in connection with the history of his friend and first victim, the king Vikar, himself incidental. The redaction which we read dates undoubtedly from the thirteenth or even the fourteenth century, but all are agreed that it faithfully records ancient material, and in particular that what it adds to the poem which it quotes and explicates, the *Víkarsbálkr*, is no gratuitous invention, but knowledge correctly transmitted.

The other document is found in the *Gesta Danorum* of Saxo Grammaticus[2] (born ca. 1150, died after 1216). It follows the life, or rather the three complete lives, of Starcatherus, divided among books VI (chapters 5 to 8), VII (chapter 5 and 11), and VIII (chapters 6 and 8). These three were, according to the plausible opinion of Paul Herrmann,[3] almost the last to be composed among the first nine, or "mythological books." The text is broken up by numerous poems, some in epic, others in lyric meters, which are all attributed to the hero and are surely paraphrases of Old Icelandic poems. Saxo's sources cannot be determined, but there is no doubt that he worked from one or more sagas, written or oral, of which there remains no trace. The problem is to know to what extent he understood them, and also to what degree he willfully modified them. In the part corresponding to the episode of the *Gautrekssaga*, Saxo is very summary, and the two accounts diverge on important points.

[2] The *Gesta Danorum* is quoted in the edition of H. R. Ellis Davison, as translated by Peter Fisher under the title, *History of the Danes* (Totowa, N.J., 1979). On Saxo, see the introduction to *From Myth to Fiction: The Saga of Hadingus*, trans. Derek Coltman (Chicago and London, 1973).

[3] These books, certainly later than the "historical books" X–XVI (from Harald Bluetooth, 936–986, to Knud VI, 1182–1202), were probably composed between 1202 and 1216 in the order: III, IV, V; VI, VII, II, I, VIII; IX.

The legend has been abundantly commented upon. One finds mention and occasional discussion of works before 1921 in Paul Herrmann's *Erläuterungen zu den ersten neun Büchern der dänischen Geschichte des Saxo Grammaticus*, 1. Teil, Kommentar (1922), pp. 417–467, 488 (mention of the second *facinus*), 522–555, 557–568. Herrmann himself made a new and careful commentary, though marred by the tendency to deny a priori the unity of the whole and to dismember the interpretation to an extreme degree. Thereafter, the principal studies have been: Herrmann Schneider, *Germanische Heldensage*, II, 1 (1933), 143–183; Jan de Vries, "Die Starkadsage," *Germanisch-Romanische Monatsschrift*, 36 (= N. F. 5 [1955]), 281–297; the second part of my *Aspects de la fonction guerrière* (1956), with, as an appendix, a summary of de Vries' article (repeated, slightly modified and without this discussion, in *The Destiny of the Warrior* [1970], part II); de Vries' clarifications in his review of *Aspects . . .*, *Beiträge zur Geschichte der deutschen Sprache und Literatur*, 78 (1957), 458–471; Edward O. G. Turville Petre, *Myth and Religion of the North* (1964), pp. 205–211.[4]

The comparative study which is presented here, if it is correct, considerably changes the standing, the very data of the problem. Let us follow first, piece by piece, the legend of Starkaðr in its several variants, and see what can be suggested, if not demonstrated, by internal criticism.

[4] Earlier bibliography, of only historical interest, will be found in Hermann Schneider's book. The old study of Johann Ludwig Uhland, naturalistic as it is, remains nonetheless one of the most interesting: *Der Mythus von Thôr nach nordischen Quellen* (1836), reprinted in Uhland's *Schriften zur Geschichte der Dichtung und Sage*, VI, ed. Adelbert von Keller (1868), 101–110. One may still profitably consider Karl Müllenhoff, *Deutsche Altertumskunde* V (2d ed. [1907] by Max Roediger), 301–356; Gustav Neckel, *Beiträge zur Eddaforschung, mit Exkursen zur Heldensage* (1908), 351–358; Axel Olrik, *Danmarks Heltedigtning*, II, *Starkad den gamle og den yngre Skjoldungrække* (1910), with Andreas Heusler's very weak (especially p. 180) review in *Anzeiger für deutsches Altertum und deutsche Literatur*, XXXV, 3 (1911), 169–183.

2. THE BIRTH, FATE, AND FIRST CRIME OF STARKAÐR

The author responsible for the episode inserted in the *Gautrekssaga* knows two characters named Starkaðr. The first, grandfather of the hero, was a monstrous giant, possessed of four pairs of arms. He abducted a certain girl, and her father appealed to the god Thor to rescue her. Thor slew the kidnapper and restored the girl to her father. But she was pregnant, and bore a handsome boy with black hair, an entirely human being who inherited from his father an extraordinary strength, and who received the name of Stórvirkr. He married a princess of Halogaland, and had by her a son whom he named, according to custom, after his grandfather, Starkaðr.

As the death of King Vikar is all that the author of the episode intends to recount, he stresses the relationship Starkaðr and Vikar had from their early youth. Stórvirkr was killed by Haraldr, king of Agðir, who brought up little Starkaðr along with his own son, Vikar. Haraldr was defeated and slain in his turn by Herthjófr, king of Hördaland, who took hostage the sons of a number of important personages, beginning with the young Vikar. One of Herthjófr's men, Grani, also called Hrosshársgrani (Horse-hair Grani), who lived in Hördaland on the island of Fenhring, took away with him as booty Starkaðr, aged three. The child stayed nine years with Grani and grew big and strong as a giant. He then helped his friend Vikar to reconquer his realm, and joined up with him, accompanying him on many victorious expeditions and being showered by him with honors.[5]

But someone had dark designs on the two friends: Odin, the sovereign god. Odin in fact destined King Vikar to be offered to him as victim in a human sacrifice, and he had chosen Starkaðr to be the sacrificer. If, from the point of view of men, the act which Starkaðr is to commit is contemptible and treasonous, one ought to refrain from being equally harsh from the god's perspective and should not mourn for Vikar. The fate of a human victim offered

[5] Chap. 3, p. 12; cf. *Saga Heidreks konungs ins vitra*, ed. Christopher Tolkien (1960), appendix ("U-Redaktion"), pp. 66–67.

to Odin, especially by hanging and spear-thrust, is not lamentable; it will honorably increase, in the otherworld, the vast body of Einherjar, who do not find the time long either in the mead-halls of Valhalla where they are the guests of the god, or on the nearby fields where between banquets they wage fierce combat, henceforth without risk. Sacrifice to Odin was as good as death on the battlefield, which every well-born German wished for. So true is this that the Scandinavians had devised a sort of sacrament designed to save by a shortcut those who had the mischance to meet with a natural death, by old age or illness: the historicized account which the *Heimskringla* (*Ynglingasaga*) gives of the reign of "king" Óðinn says that he instituted a "mark of the spear," a scratch that, inflicted on a dying man, would vouchsafe him the eternal happiness which normally ought to result only from a mortal blow received from an enemy. A warrior or king sacrificed to the god, willingly or otherwise, was assured *a fortiori* of a bountiful and violent afterlife. As for the murder which Odin is going to make Starkaðr commit, not only will it have no grievous consequences for the hero, either in this world or the next, but the god vests his command in a series of such conspicuous benefits that one is tempted to doubt its criminal character, stated though it be. Here then is how he goes about it, or rather has long since gone about it.[6]

The Hrossharsgrani who has taken to himself and brought up Starkaðr with so much solicitude and success is none other than a human form assumed by the god. Patiently, this Mentor awaits favorable circumstances to ask of his Telemachus the act for which he has thus chosen him. The moment arrives in chapter VII,[7] when, during a Viking expedition, Vikar's sailing fleet is long becalmed near a small island, and the duration of this embarrassment is such that the king and his companions resort to a magical consultation to determine the cause of it. The answer is that Odin desires a man of the army to be sacrificed to him by hanging. Lots are drawn, and

[6] Chaps. 3–6, pp. 13–27.
[7] Pp. 28–31.

it is the king who is chosen. The army remains silent and postpones the deliberations to the next day. It is indeed no minor matter to kill one's king, even in sacrifice, and besides how are they to induce Vikar, who is master of the expedition and free to forgo it, to offer himself as victim to assure a success which will no longer concern him?

It is at this point that Hrossharsgrani intervenes. In the middle of the night he awakens Starkaðr, takes him in a boat to the shore of the islet and leads him through the forest to a clearing where a strange *þing*, or assembly, is being held. A crowd of beings of human appearance are gathered around twelve high seats, eleven of which are already occupied by the chief gods. Revealing himself for who he is, Odin ascends the twelfth seat and announces that the order of business is the determination of the fate of Starkaðr. In fact, the event comes down to a magical-oratorical duel between Odin and Thor. Thor, taking the floor immediately, declares that he cannot bear good will toward a young man whose grandfather was a giant whom he had had to kill and whose grandmother, in her girlhood, had preferred this giant to him—to him, Thor, the "Thor of the Æsir"! Concluding, he imposes a first fate, a bad one: "Starkaðr will have no children."[8] Odin formulates a compensation: "Starkaðr will have three human life spans."[9] But Thor rejoins: "He will commit a villainy, a *níðingsverk*, in each."[10] And the duel continues: "He will always," says Odin, "have the best arms and the best raiments." "He will have," says Thor, "neither land nor real property." Odin: "He will have fine furnishings." Thor: "He will never feel he has enough." Odin: "He will have success and victory in every combat." Thor: "He will receive a grave wound in every combat." Odin: "He will have the gift of poetry and improvisation." Thor: "He will forget all he has composed." Odin:

[8] *"Álfhildr, móðir föður Starkaðs, kaus föður at syni sínum hundvísan jötun heldr enn Ásaþór ok skapa ek þat Starkaði, at hann skal hvórki eiga son né dóttur, ok enda svó ætt sína.*

[9] *"Þat skapa ek honum, at hann skal lifa þrjá manzaldra."*

[10] *"Hann skal vinna níðingsverk á hverjum mannzaldri."* The theme of the three *níðingsverk* was transferred to the sword Tyrfingr and its owner Svafrlámi in the *Hervararsaga* (2, p. 3 [see above, p. 9 n. 1]).

"He will appeal to the well-born and the great." Thor: "He will be despised by the common folk."

The blueprint for the future ends here. The gods endorse without discussion the propositions of the two debaters, the meeting is adjourned, and Hrosshársgrani brings Starkaðr back towards the ships. In payment for the aid he has just provided him, he demands of Starkaðr bluntly that he "send" him the king, that is arrange for the king to place himself in a position to be sacrificed: he himself will take care of the rest. Starkaðr, realizing that he must pay, agrees. And the god turns over to the man, hereafter his accomplice, a spear, telling him "that it would appear as a stick of reed" (*reyrspróti*).

> The next morning, the king's counsellors met and arrived at the following decision: they would carry out a mock sacrifice, and it was Starkaðr who proposed the plan. There stood near them a fir tree and a high stump near the fir; far down from the tree stretched a slender branch, which rose up into the foliage. The servants were preparing food for the men, and a calf had been opened and gutted. Starkaðr had them take out the calf's intestine, then he stood up on the stump, bent down the thin branch, and knotted the entrail around it. Then Starkaðr said to the king, "Your gallows is ready for you, king, and it does not seem very dangerous. Now come hither, and I will lay the rope around your neck." The king said, "If this apparatus is no more dangerous than it looks to me, then I think it will not harm me, but if it is otherwise, then it is for fate to decide what will happen." Then he stood up on the stump, and Starkaðr laid the noose around his neck and stepped down from the stump. Then Starkaðr thrust his stick at the king and said, "Now I give thee to Odin."[11] Then Starkaðr released the branch. The reed-stick suddenly became a spear and pierced the king. The stump fell out from beneath his feet, and the calf's intestine became a strong withy, and the branch sprang up and dragged the king into the leaves, and there he died. Thereafter the place has been called Víkarsholmar, 'Vikar's

[11] *"Nú gef ek þik Óðni."*

Island.' From this deed Starkaðr became much despised by the people, and was exiled from Hördaland.

Starkaðr then goes to Sweden, where he is supposed to have composed the end of the *Víkarsbálkr*,[12] and we hear nothing more of his life; it was of no further interest to the *sagamaðr*.

From the birth of Starcatherus to the death of Wicarus, Saxo's account is brief. Here it is in its entirety (Fisher, p. 170):

> In those days there was a man Starcatherus, son of Storwercus, who, when he and his comrades were involved in a disastrous shipwreck, was the only one to escape through strength or luck. On account of his wonderful pre-eminence of mind and body he was invited by Frotho to be his guest. After he had been his companion for some while and been treated more elegantly and handsomely each day, he was at length given a splendid ship and told to pursue the life of an adventurer, at the same time exercising watch over the seas. Nature had equipped him with a superhuman physique and spiritual endowments to match, so that men believed that in bravery he was second to none. So widespread was his conspicuous renown that even today his deeds and name remain distinguished in popular esteem. The roll of his achievements not only scintillated in our own country but gained him brilliant repute even through all the provinces of Sweden and Saxony.
>
> Certainly it is recorded that he came from the region which borders eastern Sweden, that which contains the wide-flung dwellings of the Estlanders and other numerous savage hordes. But a common tale has been invented about his origin which is fictitious, unreasonable and downright incredible. For some folk tell how he was born of giants and revealed his monster kind by an extraordinary number of hands. They assert that the god Thor broke the sinews which joined four of these superfluous extensions of freakish Nature and tore them off, plucking away the unatural bunches of fingers from the body

[12] Pp. 31–34.

> proper; with only two arms left, his frame, which before had run to a gigantic enormity and been shaped with a grotesque crowd of limbs, was afterwards corrected according to a better model and contained within the more limited dimensions of men.

This birth is followed in abrupt fashion by a digression into mythology, concerning in particular the gods Othinus and Thor (pp. 170–71). They were of course not "gods," Saxo explains, but magicians who by their prestige had convinced the simple folk that they were gods, and this deception had infected Norway, Sweden and Denmark. This is why their names appear in the days of the week, just as the ancient Romans had also named these days after the gods or the seven planets.

> An outcome of this is that the days of the week, in their appointed series, are thought of under the names of these "gods," since the ancient Romans are known to have given them separate titles from the names of their deities or from the seven planets. One gathers plainly from this very nomenclature of days that the persons who were honored by our people were not the same as those the early Romans called Jupiter and Mercury, or those whom Greece and Italy accorded all the homage of superstition. What we call Thor's or Odin's day is termed by them Jove's or Mercury's day. If we accept that Thor is Jupiter and Odin Mercury, following the change of the days' designations, then it is clear proof that Jupiter was the son of Mercury, if we abide by the assertions of our countrymen, whose common belief is that Thor was the child of Odin. As the Romans hold to the opposite opinion that Mercury was born of Jupiter, it follows that if their claim is undisputed, we must realize that Thor and Jupiter, Odin and Mercury are different personages.

Saxo then resumes his account as abruptly as he had interrupted it:

> Ancient tradition says that Starcatherus, whom I introduced earlier, devoted his initial career to pleasing the gods through the murder of Wicarus, king of Norway. Some narrate this

version of the affair: Othinus once desired that Wicarus should come to a dismal end, but did not wish to effect this openly. He therefore made Starcatherus, already remarkable for his unusual size, famous for his courage and his artistry in composing spells, so that he could use the man's energies more readily to accomplish the king's death. Othinus hoped that this was how Starcatherus would show his thanks for the privileges bestowed on him. To this end he also gave him three times the span of mortal life, in order that he might perpetrate a proportionate number of damnable deeds, and crime accompany his prolonged existence.

He soon came to Wicarus and for some time lodged with him in his palace, devising a trap during his attendance on the king.

Eventually they embarked together on a pirating expedition but arrived at a place where they were troubled by a long spell of violent storms. The gales interrupted their voyage and made them spend a major part of the year doing nothing, till they decided that the gods must be appeased by human blood. Lots cast in an urn showed a demand for a royal victim. Starcatherus then twined round the king's neck a noose he had made of osier, pretending to offer the appearance of an expiation merely for a moment. But the tightness of the knot fulfilled its function and cut short Wicarus' breathing as he hung there. While he was still panting Starcatherus tore out the remnants of life with his sword, and when he should have lent relief disclosed his treachery. I cannot entertain the view of one version which relates that the soft osiers hardened as they suddenly gripped and acted like a halter of iron.[13]

Once this first crime has been committed, Starcatherus associates himself with a Danish Viking. At first with him, and later alone, he travels over a huge area: Russia, Ruthenia, Biarmia, Sweden, Ireland, Slavia, Russia again, Byzantium, Poland, Saxony, and eventually arrives at the court of the Danish king Frotho (pp.

[13] Saxo did not understand the two-staged scenario of the sacrifice; see *The Destiny of the Warrior*, trans. Alf Hiltebeitel (Chicago and London, 1970), p. 91, and nn. 7, 8.

172–174). Everywhere he performs outstanding exploits, a model of martial virtue.

3. ODIN, THOR AND STARKAÐR IN THE GAUTREKSSAGA AND IN SAXO

The two tales, the Icelandic and the Latin, follow in the main the same pattern but manifest significant differences on several points. And as happens whenever a comparison is made on the basis of only two terms, it is difficult to unravel a single archetype of which the known texts would be two divergent derivatives. Aside from the fact that it is not even certain that such an archetype ever existed—folklorists are accustomed to discovering such irreducible doublets—it is inevitable, whatever effort the critic may make at objectivity, that in arguing from one probability to the next he may venture beyond what is justifiable. In this case, however, internal criticism does lead to some conclusions.

The presentation of the birth of Starkaðr is tighter in Saxo than in the saga. Saxo knows only a single Starcatherus, who consolidates what the saga distributes between the two Starkaðrs, grandfather and grandson: his native monstrosity, the intervention of the gods, and the beginning of his heroic career. This discrepancy, while at first seeming considerable, is nonetheless reduced by the fact that, according to the *Víkarsbálkr*, the grandson bears hereditary traces of his grandfather's monstrosity, vestigial stumps of supernumerary arms. I know that those critics who are quick to prune the texts, and to reject as later additions whatever does not fit their idea of the "original" plot, have edited out the stanza of the poem which says this in clear terms;[14] their reasons are very weak. If one avoids mutilating the *bálkr*, the Icelandic and Latin versions are not so different, since even in the former Starkaðr is not, even

[14] Stanzas 31–32 (= 36–37 of the saga):

31. *Séa þykkjask þeir / á sjálfum mér / jötunkuml / átta handa, //*
er Hlorriði / fyr hamar norðan / Hergríms bana / höndum rænti.

at his beginnings, such a handsome young man as one could hardly believe to have been descended from a monstrous giant. On the contrary, because of this origin he is at birth very like Starcatherus "retouched" by Thor, and like him carries stigmata, *jötunkuml*: stumps or vestiges of undeveloped limbs, if not scars of amputated ones.

Under these circumstances, it is impossible to guess which of the two variants preserves the original state. The *lectio* of Saxo is hardly *difficilior* than that of the saga and both, in different ways, recall the type of the hero relieved of superfluous arms (in Saxo by direct amputation; in the saga amputation with hereditary transmission of the "acquired characteristic," but a trace of the old state). But this type is without parallel in all the heroic tales of the North, and this is undoubtedly the most important fact. One is inclined at first to think that it is the saga which, to reduce the strangeness of the type without eliminating it, divided it into two stages, over two separate generations, and that Saxo has preserved in this instance a purer and simpler datum. However, when one reflects on the liberties which Saxo or his immediate source have taken in many other cases where they are easily discovered, one hesitates to attribute such fidelity to him here. Moreover, in a fragment of a poem much older (tenth century) than the *Gautrekssaga*, four lines of the skald Vetrliði Sumarliðason (the only ones pre-

---

32. *Hlæja menn / er mik séa / ljótan skolt / langa trjónu //*
hár úlfgrátt / hangar tjálgur / hrúfan háls / húð jótraða.

31. ". . . They [i.e. the Swedes, with whom Starkaðr has taken refuge] think they see upon myself the giant's mark, eight arms, where Hlorriði [= Thor] . . . relieved Hergrím's bane of his arms. 32. Men laugh when they see me, ugly jaw, long snout, wolf-gray hair, hanging arms, scarred neck, wrinkled skin."

Cf. Ranisch, in his introduction to the *Gautrekssaga* (above, p. 9, n. 1), p. xcvii [translated from German]: "The men of the Swedish kings still wished to find on Starkaðr marks of his gigantic descent, traces of eight arms, as that older Starkaðr had, the killer of Hergrímr"; Paul Herrmann, *Kommentar*, p. 423: "Like a mark of Cain he bears the signs of gigantic extraction on his body, the stumps of the eight arms which Thor removed from his grandfather, the wild look, the wolfish snout."

served of his work), Starkaðr is named in a list of giants who came to grief at the hands of the god Thor:

> You broke the legs of Leikn,
> thrashed Thrívaldi,
> overthrew Starkaðr,
> caused the death of Gjölp.[15]

The violent, hostile act designated by the verb *steypa* (to throw [hurl] down, to overthrow), can scarcely be that by which the Thor of Saxo "contains Starcatherus within the more limited dimensions of men." It is rather that by which Thor, in the saga, slays the first Starkaðr.

The differences become more serious when we consider the role of the gods in the tales of Starkaðr's birth (the monster reduced to human limits) and the murder of Vikar. For here it is the gods who direct the action, free to disappear afterward and to disinterest themselves, at least apparently, in the career they have arranged for the hero.

Here again, Saxo is simpler and seems more coherent. The two gods step in successively, without interference; and soberly, each one with a single gift, or with several, which do not call for any response. Thor first of all brings the young Starcatherus to human form, and this act seems to be understood by Saxo as a good deed, since out of a horrible giant he has made a man, offering him the chance of a useful and illustrious existence. Only thereafter does Othinus appear. As he needs to obtain from Starcatherus a service which, from the human point of view, is an abominable crime, a *facinus*, the murder of the king his master and friend, he pays generously: all the physical and spiritual qualities that will make an exceptional hero; poetic skill, by which the hero will also be the first great skald; and a life extended to the length of three normal

[15] Ernst Albin Kock, *Den norsk-isländska Skaldedigtningen* (1946), I, 71:

> *leggi brauzt Leiknar,*
> *lamðir þrívalda,*
> *steypðir Starkeði,*
> *stétt of Gjölp dauða.*

human lives. In this presentation of "gifts," though, there is a problem: Othinus has need of only the first *facinus*, the murder of Wicarus, but he burdens the gift of three lives with threefold servitude: Starcatherus will commit three *facinora*, one in each life. Why? We might answer, being modern comparativists, that the saga was composed on the traditional theme of the "three functional sins of the warrior," and the three *facinora* have been imposed at the cost of a certain ungainliness in composition.[16] But this would be to give little credit to the skill of the *sagamenn*. One is led to believe rather that on this point Saxo has slightly altered a more satisfactory original.

Moreover, if the interventions of Thor and Othinus are successive and without any element of rivalry or conflict, one point in Saxo's composition arouses suspicion, namely the parallelism of the two gods, of their natures and their Latin interpretations, which, placed as it is between the birth and the career of the hero, constitutes a parenthesis within the story and interrupts it to no advantage. For what advantage is there in defining two gods in this way, one in terms of the other, in opposition to each other, when their interventions are entirely independent and not even complementary? But this is a common practice of Saxo, well illustrated and clarified particularly by the "saga of Hadingus," in the first book of the *Gesta Danorum*.[17]

Hadingus is the god Njörðr transposed into a Viking hero. Such transfer requires some fancy footwork, granted the essentially peaceful character of Njörðr in the mythology (such moreover is the fate of all the divinities, including that other "pacifist" Baldr, whom Saxo has enlisted in his first nine books, the "mythological books," to provide a prehistory for his Danish history). But it was impossible for any Scandinavian mythographer at all to speak of Njörðr, his life and lineage, without mentioning the distinction and

[16] See above, pp. 1–8.

[17] *From Myth to Fiction* (1973), chap. 6 ("The first mythological digression: giants, Ase gods and Vane gods") and 7 ("The second mythological digression: the war between the Ases and the Vanes").

opposition of the Æsir and the Vanir, and even their primeval war. For it is at the conclusion of this war, by virtue of the peace treaty, that the great Vanir gods—Njörðr, Freyr, Freyja—become the partners of the Æsir, members with them in a joint community. More particularly, this war marks a turning point in Njörðr's life: hitherto purely Van (with an incestuous marriage), thereafter Van retouched according to the "morality" of the Æsir (with a new, nonincestuous marriage). As all his characters were human, Saxo, who in this circumstance seems moreover to have understood poorly the pagan theology of the ancient Scandinavians, could not transpose as such these divisions of supernatural beings. Nevertheless he has not let them slip away. In two places, at the beginning where the mythology imposed a contrastive definition of the Æsir and the Vanir, and later, at the turn where the mythology presented the war and the reconciliation of the two divine groups, Saxo inserted two disquisitions, one theological, the other mythological, long and ungainly parentheses unrelated to the narrative, matching with evident awkwardness these two fundamental strands of the protonarrative.

It is probably likewise in the story of Starcatherus. If Saxo has inserted here a contrastive definition of Thor and of Othinus which is in no way necessary to the action as he describes it, it is undoubtedly because, in the Scandinavian saga of Starkaðr which he used, the character opposition between Thor and Odin on the contrary played at this point an important role. Consequently the Danish "historian" has here modified and simplified the unknown *sagamaðr*'s account, eliminating from the plot a specific example of the rivalry of the two gods and replacing it with a general theory.

To be sure, it can be objected that Saxo's account does in fact present an opposition in the behaviors of the two gods toward the hero, and that this is enough to motivate their confrontation in the form of a theological digression. Thor's action is wholly good, with no noxious pendant, while that of Othinus is nastily ambivalent and Saxo's very wording reveals that it is because he needs the first crime that he is so interested in the hero. Nonetheless, Thor does not directly or actively oppose Othinus here, for example he does not intervene to defend his erstwhile protégé against this evil lot.

There is another difficulty besides this one.[18] The role of Othinus agrees with what Scandinavian tradition says of Odin. As sovereign god, he grants gifts which amount to "lots," that is, he determines a destiny. A complex, disquieting, maleficent god, he compounds this destiny out of "good" privileges mingled with an "evil" demand. That he is interested in Starcatherus, a giant by birth, a humanized giant, is not surprising either: more than one trait of the ambiguous Odin, beginning with his ancestry, connects him with that race. In contrast the role Saxo has Thor play is unique. In every circumstance this god is the irreconcilable enemy of all giants; he slays those who venture among the Æsir and goes off to kill others in their own haunts, the land of the giants being the normal stage of his exploits. But on meeting a young giant who, to make matters worse, is marked by the monstrosity of six arms, which make him three times as dangerous, he does not kill him. Having him at his mercy, not only does he not destroy him, but he performs a series of surgical operations which make him normal. This unique failing of Thor in his calling remains unexplained; Saxo is here suspect a priori of having misunderstood or altered a version of the story in which Thor remained faithful to himself—which, it should be said in passing, seems to indicate that for the birth, the Icelandic version is preferable.

If the account of the saga is more satisfactory with regard to the theology, however, it still has difficulties of its own. Thor and Odin oppose, even confront each other, at the assembly of the gods, in the conflict in which young Starkaðr is the pawn. Thor is consistently hostile, Odin consistently benevolent. Thor's hostility has two causes, the first of which is completely in line with his character. Because the first Starkaðr was of the race of giants, which he abhors, he has not "tailored," but killed him; and he

[18] What follows is the revision of my earlier proposals (cf. above, pp. 5–6), as given in *The Destiny of the Warrior*, p. 83 n. 1 (cf. p. 95 n. 11).

naturally extends his hatred to the grandson, even though the latter, apart from the "marks" of the extra arms which heredity has imposed on him, is a man. The second cause is more surprising, at least in one of the two successive descriptions which the *Gautreks-saga* provides. Chapter III recounts nothing abnormal: the giant, following the custom of his race, has abducted a young woman, apparently without her consent. Her father requests the help of Thor, who wipes out the abductor and returns the victim to her family, the victim who thereafter carries in her womb the father of the saga's hero. With good reason this vengeful action of Thor has been compared with certain exploits attributed to him by the mythology; more than one giant has succumbed under his hammer for having abducted or threatened to abduct a fair goddess. But in chapter VII, when Thor states his grievances in the gods' assembly, he speaks of something else: the girl has had to "choose," *kjósa,* as in an Indian *svayaṃvara,* and she has preferred (*kaus . . . heldr en . . .*) the giant to the god. And to what a god, to him, the "Thor of the Æsir"! If Thor has killed the giant, it was in punishment for this presumptuousness; he has simply gone about it a little late, when the girl was already, so to speak, with the interpolation of a son, pregnant with her grandson, the second Starkaðr. Thus Thor, to put an end to this evil brood, must above all condemn the young Starkaðr, at the fixing of his fate, to have neither son nor daughter, *hvórki eiga son né dóttur*. This romantic rivalry between a giant and Thor, and generally the notion of "loves of Thor," are extraordinary, even if pride rather than sentiment seems to motivate the god here. Still we should avoid the too-hasty conclusion that this romanesque element is the late invention of a *sagamaðr.* In any case let us note that, thus imposed by Thor, the curse of the three *níðingsverk* is comprehensible. Since Odin has granted the hero three lives, Thor, with nothing really specific in mind, ordains three crimes. This was not the case, one should remember, in Saxo where Othinus, who needs only one *facinus* of Starcatherus, nevertheless foretells and imposes three misdeeds.

The relationships between Odin and Starkaðr in the saga are at once simpler and more complex than in Saxo. Simpler because, in the scene where the two gods, in a sort of stichomachy, oppose each other in determining the character and the fate of the hero, all the good is furnished by Odin, and all the bad, as might be expected from a steadfast grudge, is imposed by Thor. More complex and, all things considered, harder to understand because on the one hand, Odin's kindness toward Starkaðr leads to his demand on him, forcing Starkaðr to commit a great crime which will dishonor him, and on the other, this crime is the result of a strange and peculiar collusion of the hatred of Thor and need of Odin.

With the exception of Thor's curse, in fact, the conduct of Odin and the development of the plot are logical: Odin has long ago, from Starkaðr's childhood, chosen him to officiate at the sacrifice of Vikar. In view of this he has made the youth indebted to him, at first by raising him and making him an eminent hero, later, at the time of the contradictory imposition of his fate, by piling up in his presence the "good" prescriptions. All that remains for Odin is to present his due statement, and this is in fact how he makes use of the gifts: *Vel muntu nú launa mér,* "Now you must repay me for the education, *fóstri,* and the help, *liðsemd,* that I have given you." And Starkaðr is so indebted, perhaps also so attached to his foster father, that he makes no objection. *Vel, sagði Starkaðr. . . .*

The intervention of Thor disturbs this arrangement. For if it is Odin who decides that the hero will live three human lives, *at hava skal lifa þrjá mannzaldra,* it is Thor who, rejoining that the hero will commit a villainy in each, *hann skal vinna níðingsverk á hverjum mannzaldri,* announces, authorizes, renders truly inevitable the criminal act which Odin will demand of Starkaðr, which he has been arranging for so many years, and whose immediate conditions he has already gathered just before the scene of the assembly of the gods (lack of wind making sailing impossible, presence of a tree and a stump "naturally" suited for a mock hanging). How is this apparent contradiction to be understood? Strictly speaking, one might think that, after Odin has arranged the material conditions for the crime in which he will engage Starkaðr, he desires to share the responsibility with others (though this would not be customary for him), to be somehow morally covered by a collective decision of the gods: hence this *þing*, this general assembly of the highest deities which is held, miraculously enough, exactly on an islet close by the immobilized fleet. But how comes it that Thor gives Odin precisely what Odin has come to seek? Shall we admit a complicity between these two gods who seem so antagonistic? The story as a whole excludes it. Should one suppose that, in his omniscience, Odin has foreseen that Thor would fling the curse of the "three villainies"? The idea is gratuitous. Or rather more subtly, has the crafty, Machiavellian Odin manipulated Thor, a character all of a piece, a model of uncompromising honor, as the toreador "works" the bull, announcing the gift of "three lives" only to draw out the response "with a dishonor in each"? But besides the fact that Thor's response could have been different (three great misfortunes, three physical setbacks, etc.), it is not in fact Odin but Thor who at this point in the debate runs the show and leads the discussion. The gift of the "three lives" by Odin is simply the compensation or counterpart for Thor's first curse: Thor has said that Starkaðr will have no descendants; so be it, says Odin, but he himself will live the span of three generations. And it is only then, to rebut this rebuttal, that Thor makes his second curse, that of the three villainies. In fact, no explanation is satisfactory, and however one attempts to unravel it, the tangle is unresolved; perhaps the *sagamaðr* has altered, complicated the traditional material?

One might hope for some illumination from the more ancient poem intercalated in the saga, on which the prose account is only a commentary. But the elliptical, rhetorical character of this *Víkarsbálkr* makes even its most precise expressions leave room for doubt. Indeed, in this confession or plea which he makes after the crime before the hostile and derisive assembly of the Swedish noblemen, Starkaðr expressly imputes to Thor the responsibility for the murder of Vikar, alluding to the curse of the three *níðingsverk*:[19]

Þess eyrindis
at Þórr um skóp
mér níðings nafn,

[19] Stanza 26 (= 31 of the saga).

. . .
hlaut ek óhróðigr
illt at vinna.

"On such a mission,
when Thor assigned me
the name of villain . . .
I was forced without glory
to do evil."

And in the following stanza, it is a *pluralis pudicitiae*—"the gods"—that masks Odin, his will and initiative:

Skyllda ek Víkar
í viði háfum
Geirþjófsbana
goðum um signa;
lagða ek geiri
gram til hjarta
þat er mér harmazt
handaverka.

"Vikar I had
in a high tree,
Geirthjóf's bane,
to consign to the gods;
I set the spear
to the hero's heart.
That to me was the most grievous
of my hands' deeds."

Thus, in the operetta, La Belle Hélène indicts fate, forgetting both her own will and the initiative of the Trojan prince. Starkaðr emphasizes the sad "lot" cast by Thor, and glosses over all that has followed, between the curse and its first result. But this obviously tendentious presentation does not acquit Odin any more than it absolves Starkaðr himself, and it does not attest, as one has sometimes thought, a third variant in which Odin has nothing at all to do with the affair and it is solely and directly Thor who has imposed and orchestrated the crime. Furthermore the mention made in an earlier stanza (8, = 3) of Hrosshársgrani does not permit such an easy exclusion of the great sovereign god. Hrossharsgrani is certainly Odin both in the poem and in the prose narrative, and his solicitude for Starkaðr there cannot be more disinterested.

Through these difficulties and even contradictions, and whether one posits at the source a single variant which Saxo would have very considerably altered and the Scandinavian texts better preserved, or rather two already perceptibly different variants, there remains nonetheless a reasonably clear pattern, uniform but with two alternatives.

1. Starkaðr is either a giant with many arms, reduced by Thor to "human measure," or the homonymous grandson of a many-armed giant slain by Thor, bearing the physical traces of this monstrous descent.

2. Two antagonistic divinities intervene at his beginnings:

a) Saxo's plot, which reduces this antagonism, *in excursu*, to a theological discussion with no effect on the outcome, also reduces the intervention of Thor to the initial benevolent, beneficent operation by which he makes a normal man out of this monstrous giant. The bestowal of all "lots," both good and bad, is reserved for Othinus, moreover the evil lots are reduced to one, that of the three *facinora* which encumber the three *vitae* and of which the first is immediately necessary to Othinus.

b) In the saga, the antagonism is active, and expressed at length at the fixing of Starkaðr's fate. The two gods wrangle over the hero, one wishing to make him happy, the other ill-starred, and then the first crime is committed, which Odin needs and has prepared long since, but which, since it involves *fatum*, is decided on by Thor at the moment of its implementation.

4. THE FACINORA, STARCATHERUS AND THE KINGS

The balance of the story, from the aftermath of the first *facinus* to the perpetration of the third, presents no difficulty. The essentials have been mentioned above, and it seems that Saxo, from here on our only source, has fully understood and respected the

Scandinavian tradition, which has not come down to us in the vernacular but which certainly existed, since the proclamation of the three *níðingsverk* in the *Gautrekssaga* makes sense only if the second and third, as well as the first, were eventually carried out. Starcatherus, then, passes his three human life spans in a continuous aging process—shortly after the episode of the murder of Wicarus Saxo already calls him *senex*—but he keeps all his strength, at least until the third *facinus*, until the combined effect of his privileged longevity and the immoral condition burdening him has run its course.

The terrible, mutilating wounds which he receives in several combats, and the enmity which he displays repeatedly towards common folk (except farmers), correspond to two items in the curse which Thor imposes on Starkaðr in the *Gautrekssaga*, items which Saxo has not preserved as such but whose existence in his source material is proven here by their realization. Roughly, this career is a series of extraordinary exploits, against the barbarians in the East and the aggressive neighbors of the Scandinavians. It unfolds in the service of Swedish and Danish kings toward whom the hero displays unblemished loyalty and devotion which he readily shifts to the sons upon the death of the fathers. Simply, just as he once helped Odin to kill his first master and childhood friend, King Vikar, twice more he fails peculiarly in his duty, impelled by the lot that has been cast for him. The second *facinus* is a shameful flight when the Swedish army, in whose ranks he is fighting, has been shaken by the death of its king; the third, the most vile, is the putting to death, in exchange for money, of a Danish king, who though not very admirable is still no less his master.

It is remarkable that the three *facinora*, whose content Othinus in Saxo and Thor in the *Gautrekssaga* leave completely undefined, should all be realized in the same area: the relationships of the hero with kings, his successive masters. He might have allowed himself many other dishonorable excesses, but the two murders which he commits are those of kings who trust him, and his flight on the battlefield immediately upon the death of his king—a usurper, but no matter—is a failure in a very serious posthumous duty to the king, to ensure the passage of power to the legitimate heir, a duty to which in other circumstances he adheres, for example in returning from Denmark to Sweden to install on the throne Prince Sywardus, son of King Haldanus, "killed by his rivals" (*History of the Danes*, p. 183).

This localization of the *facinora* is explainable. It makes them especially heinous, inasmuch as they contradict what, apart from these three cases, consistently characterizes Starcatherus: an extremely lofty ideal, a kind of religion of regal worth, a true vocation as theoretician, defender, indeed tutor of royal personages and royalty *per se*. This trait is so essential to his character that it by itself justifies an episode in three parts, replete with poems and itself as long as the rest of the saga, and which if not considered from this point of view looks like a foreign body: that of the tumultuous relations of the hero with the children, daughter and son, of the fourth Frotho, a Danish king whom he served. But much earlier and more briefly, under King Frotho himself, Starcatherus had already theorized about his conduct.

In fact it is with Frotho that he had come to live after the first *facinus*. But he kept a great freedom of movement, piling up exploits from Byzantium to the subarctic country of the "Biarmians." From these long journeys he returned by chance in the nick of time, just when the poorly subjugated Saxons had personally challenged and endangered the Danish king (p. 174):

> Meanwhile the Saxons were contemplating rebellion and giving particular thought to how they could destroy Frotho, so far undefeated, in a way which would avoid a general conflict. Because they believed the most suitable method was individual combat they sent emissaries to issue a challenge to the king, aware that he always embraced every danger eagerly and that his high spirit would certainly never give way to any admonition. When they knew that Starcatherus, whose bravery intimidated most men, was occupied elsewhere, they reckoned then was the time to accost Frotho. But while the king was

hesitating and saying he would have to consult his friends about a reply, Starcatherus appeared on the scene, back from his sea-roving; he severely criticized the idea of the challenge because, as he pointed out, such fights were not appropriate for kings except against their equals and certainly they should not be undertaken against men of the people; more properly it devolved on himself, as one born in a humbler station, to handle this contest.

After this statement, which convinces the king, Starcatherus goes forward, confronts and kills the huge champion Hama, whom the Saxons had wished to set up against Frotho.

Of course the hero, devoted to his king, assessed the danger and wished to save him. But, Saxo states, this was not the most important thing for him; after all, a king as much as and more than any other warrior should be daring and risk himself, even if it be in an unequal combat. But he must not degrade himself. Symmetrically, the principal offense of the Saxons was not their revolt, nor their defiance, but their failure to honor the worth, the transcendence of kingship—there is a royal class, the *compares*, with its own rights and duties and set apart from all the rest. No more in international affairs than in his own realm must the king descend to the level of the *populares*, be they countrymen or foreigners, and no *popularis* may aspire to the level of a king, especially not with the intention of surpassing him.

The long episode of the children of Frotho (pp. 175–6) merely develops and stages the same precept in the following generation. Starcatherus is there at once a theoretician and a man of action; he teaches authoritatively and imperiously directs, so to speak, fieldwork exercises.

Frotho is dead, assassinated by a Dane named Suertingus who incidentally also perished on the same occasion, and the son of Frotho has ascended the throne. But this youth, Ingellus (Ingjaldr), behaves astonishingly. Instead of seeking to avenge his father, he weds the daughter of the murderer and makes intimates of his wife's brothers. He devotes himself to pleasures, not only in the bedchamber to the abundant sensual pleasures which his consort legitimately offers him, but also in the dining room to gluttony which is described graphically and at length, and in which appears moreover his scandalous intimacy with his messmates—his brothers-in-law, the sons of Suertingus.

Starcatherus cannot endure this spectacle of *intemperantia*. To avoid seeming to condone this dissoluteness, *luxuriae assensor*, he leaves Denmark and changes masters, entering the service of the Swedish king, Haldanus. But from Uppsala, grumbling with indignation, he watches what is happening at the court of Denmark. Admittedly weird goings-on take place there, not very compatible with the majesty of royal blood.

To begin with there is Helga (pp. 176 ff.), the nubile sister of Ingellus. This unfortunate accedes to the attentions, the familiarities, and soon the demands of a certain goldsmith, *auri faber*, one of those low-class people whom Starcatherus particularly despises, respecting only those who work the land, and among the *fabri* only those who forge weapons. No doubt proud of his wealth, this lout has Helga comb his hair, then, opening his pants, invites the young lady to delouse him.

Starcatherus sets out, with the swiftness of locomotion which seems a gift from his giant ancestry, and appears in the hall where these disgusting ministrations are taking place. Leaping at once at the goldsmith he keeps him from fleeing, cuts his buttocks to pieces with his sword, and expresses his feelings toward the two culprits in ninety-two hexameters which must be the paraphrase of a Scandinavian poem. To the young woman he is willing to concede certain extenuating circumstances, but what a sermon! The Scanian monk gives full rein to his penchant for *amplitudo*:

Defer auis, venerare patres, memor esto parentum
et proavos metire tuos, stet gloria carni.

Respect thy forebears, venerate thy ancestors,
be mindful of those who bore thee, take the measure of
thy forefathers, let renown be in thy lineage.

He showers the mutilated goldsmith with his contempt:

> *Quis furor incessit? Quod te, faber improbe, fatum*
> *impulit ingenuam tentare cupidine stirpem?*
>
> What madness got into you? What fate, wicked smith,
> propelled you to try your lust on a noble breed?

Then he returns to the daughter of Frotho:

> *Aut quis te, virgo claris dignissima fulcris,*
> *egit in obscuram Venerem? . . .*
>
> And you, maiden most worthy of an illustrious bed,
> who drove you to base love-making? . . .

But this is merely a prelude. Once the execution is done, and Helga rehabilitated, Starcatherus returns to Sweden, whence he continues to observe Denmark uncompromisingly and recrosses the straits, when he deems it necessary, with his supernatural speed. After a second "lesson" given to a well-intentioned but misguided young noble betrothed to another daughter of Frotho (pp. 179–183), there comes the third scene, the main event: Starcatherus takes on the king himself, the weakling Ingellus (pp. 183 ff.).[20]

The old hero has just installed on the Swedish throne the young Sywardus who was kept from reigning by his father's assassins, when he learns, *fama rei crebrescente*, that the horrors at the Danish court are no longer tolerable. He decides to put an end to them and sets out with a great load of charcoal on his shoulder. To all who ask, he replies that with these coals he is going to sharpen the blunted spirit of King Ingellus, *Ingelli regis hebetudinem ad acuminis habitum carbonibus se perducturum.*

He arrives in the hall where Ingellus, at first with his wife, then with her and her brothers, indulges in the most incredible excesses and refinements of gastronomy. He is unknown to and treated with disrespect by the *regina*, but is soon recognized by Ingellus and from then on surrounded with an excess of deference. But he refuses to eat, flings at the queen's head the presents which she

[20] An old form of this episode inspired a fine passage in *Beowulf*, in an entirely different plot, lines 2009–2069.

ineptly offers him, hurls a bone at the musician in charge of mollifying him, and recites to Ingellus poems of both invective and exhortation. The source of these lyric pieces is certainly, here again, one or two Scandinavian poems, but the virtuosity and zest of Saxo have no less certainly outdone the originals. In these Sapphic stanzas, twenty-one in the first poem, forty-nine in the second, the hero takes the young king to task for fraternizing with the murderers of his father instead of avenging him, for being *virtute vacuus*, abandoning himself to lust—and this in very coarse Latin, which follows for example the movements of Ingellus' hand over the most secret parts of his wife's body—and also for the gluttony which he calls *petulantis stomachi ingluvies*; but above all, overshadowing and outweighing the other ills, for not behaving like a king.

In this flood of eloquence, he refers to the youth as king only once, in the third person and with humiliating epithets, while at the same time he recalls emphatically the conduct of the *rex* Frotho and the normal demeanor of *reges* and of the assembly of kings, *contio regum*. Thus, in the first poem, he blames himself for the death of Frotho: "I should never have gone away from you, for that was your death warrant, *maxime regum*" (st. 12). "Why was I not there when a treacherous guest butchered the king, *regis iugulum petebat*?" (st. 13). "Why did I not die with the king, or avenging him, *pari gaudens sequerer beatum funere regem . . .* ?" In contrast, the new king Ingellus (st. 19):

> *Sed probum quaerens adii gulosum*
> *deditum ventri vitioque regem*
> *cuius in luxum studium refudit*
> *foeda voluptas*
>
> But seeking a virtuous king, I found a glutton,
> one given over to belly and vice,
> whose keenness has been perverted to license
> by foul lust.

The second poem develops boundlessly this theme of the degenerate king; for example, the depiction there of gluttony (st. 12):

Quis prior regum potuit gulosus
viscerum putres agitare sordes
aut manu carptim fodicare foedum
alitis anum?

What king before could be so gluttonous as to
rummage in rotten filth of bowels,
or with his hand pick and dig in
the foul anus of a bird?

And the hero-poet cries out in his anguish (st. 30–31):

Unde, cum regum tituli canuntur
et ducum vates memorant triumphos
pallio vultum pudibundus abdo
pectore tristi.

Cum tuis nil eniteat trophaeis
quod stilo digne queat adnotari
nemo Frothonis recitatur heres
inter honestos.

Therefore, when the honors of kings are sung
and poets remember the triumphs of leaders,
ashamed, I cover my face with my mantle,
saddened in heart.

Since nothing shines with your trophies
that could be worthily consigned to writing,
no heir of Frotho is counted
among the respectable.

Increasingly violent, he hammers away at Ingellus, that he might rediscover the meaning and understand the requirements of his royal function (st. 37):

Te pudor late comes insequetur
et gravi vultum feriet rubore
quando magnorum sociata ludit
contio regum . . .

Disgrace will dog you, your constant companion,
and make your face heavy with shame,

when the convened assembly of great kings
makes merry.

The miracle occurs. This time in prose, Saxo describes the youth's metamorphosis (p. 193 f.):

> At first Ingellus' ears were deaf to the song, but soon he was moved by his guardian's more urgent exhortations and his spirit, late in the day, caught the heat of revenge. He forgot the part of reveller and became an adversary. In the end he leapt from his place and unloosed the avalanche of his fury on the guests. Bloodthirsty, ruthless, he bared his sword and levelled its point at the throats of Suertingus' sons, whose palates he had been tickling with culinary delights.

And here is Saxo's commentary, in praise of a hero who is obviously close to his heart (p. 194):

> How then can we value this tireless veteran, who had stormed with his eloquent admonitions the vast corruption of the king's mind and in its place, after bursting through the barriers of immorality, had planted a most effectual seed of valor? Acting in partnership, he assisted the royal arm and not only displayed outstanding bravery himself, but summoned it back where it had been uprooted from another's bosom.

The hero recites, and is supposed to have composed for the occasion, fifty-seven hexameters, a last poetic piece, incidentally incomplete and fragmentary, which ends the sixth book and which begins with the acclamation wherein he accords Ingellus, in the vocative, the title of *rex* which he has until now refused or given only derisively:

Rex Ingelle, vale, cuius iam prodidit ausum
plenum animi pectus. . . .

King Ingellus, farewell, whose heart full of courage
has at last produced a daring deed. . . .

And he repeats the title further on, again in the vocative, to persuade the young king, who has just killed his brothers-in-law, to rid himself of their sister, his wife:

Tu quoque, rex, saevam, si quid sapis, effuge nuptam,
ne lupa consimilem sibi fetum gignat et ex te
belua consurgat proprio nocitura parenti. . . .

And you, king, if you have any sense, rid yourself of your
savage wife,
lest the she-wolf produce offspring like to herself,
and a beast arise from you to harm its own father. . . .

Thus, in a violent outburst, is expressed the basic "ideology" of Starcatherus. One sees that, behind his emotional attachment to the person and later the memory of Frotho, he in fact serves kingship as such, imperiously and didactically, a true *educator,* who draws out the young son of the great king for a kingly deed, on the accomplishment of which he awards him, one might say confers on him the title which is the object of his cult and which he has refused him only in order to deliver it with all its content and grandeur. This impassioned, aggressive defense of kingly worth is truly fundamental in his character.

With Ingellus set straight, Starcatherus can set out again with unencumbered mind for other battles, which culminate, at the beginning of the eighth book, in the famous battle of Bråvalla, the account of which he is said to have composed himself, in verse.

5. THE END OF STARCATHERUS; STARCATHERUS AND HATHERUS

Here again Saxo remains, in his Book Eight, our only authority for the account of the death of Starcatherus. The few facts for which one might have looked to local folklore—for the *Gesta Danorum* names the place where the event happened—are nothing but folklorizations from Saxo or bold, semi-scholarly assimilations from Saxo's hero and giants of local fables. No *excursus* in any saga, no allusion in a skaldic poem informs us. This paucity of information is regrettable because, as with the childhood, the monk, enamored of national traditions but poorly equipped to understand them in depth, has clearly been confused at certain points. In a word, his account is not entirely comprehensible, whether because he has juxtaposed several variants, as certain repetitions might suggest, or because he has awkwardly rationalized or simply altered his material. Let us follow him step by step.

Starcatherus, having exhausted his three lives, is now but a wreck. He who just before, despite his age, was still a champion in active service, in whom his master, King Olo, had every confidence, whom the conspirators hired for money to put an end to the reign of this dangerous tyrant, and who thereupon punished them vigorously for having bribed him, he is suddenly almost blind, supported on crutches, keeping, to be sure, enough strength to strike down anyone imprudent enough to come near him, but unable to maneuver or attack. And yet this final episode follows immediately on the murder of Olo and the punishment of the conspirators, not only temporally but logically: it is its direct consequence. If one insists on restoring some verisimilitude to the fictitious, one will admit that after the third and last prophesied *facinus*, the formula by which Othinus had conferred on him two extensions of life, having no further object, has ceased to operate, and that the hero has been suddenly marked with the scars of an extreme, triple old age.

In any case, *prolixa iam aetate defessus*, he determines that he will not die thus of *senium*, nor from illness; *egregium fore putavit, si voluntarium sibi conscisceret exitum, fatumque proprio maturasset arbitrio*, "he thought it would be honorable to embrace a voluntary end and hasten on death at his own decision." In which, Saxo remarks judiciously, he conforms to the ancient morality of the Germans, so often illustrated and implicit in the *Ynglingasaga* in the great name of Odin: *adeo quondam rei bellicae deditis morbo oppetere probrosum existimatum est*, "Dying through illness was once thought as discreditable as this by individuals who were dedicated to warfare." The old man has besides this another, more personal reason to make an end of it: the remorse of his last *facinus*, or more deeply, the feeling that with this last *facinus* his life has lost the ambiguity which gave it such special meaning. For this reason, linking his own death to that of Olo, he decides to devote the money he has shamefully received, the price of his master's blood, to buy the executioner of his choice (p. 247).

Carrying two swords and two crutches, he travels slowly and has several encounters. The first raises no difficulty; it is intended only to emphasize a feature of his character already illustrated several times in a previous episode (the mutilated goldsmith; the repulsed "saviors"), and corresponding to one of the fatal traits which Thor, according to the *Gautrekssaga*, has imposed on him, namely the incompatability of temperament which opposes him to the common people. A man of lower class, *popularium quidam*, comes near him, and thinking two swords to be too many for the hands of an old man, *geminum gladiorum usum seni supervacuum ratus*, insists that he give one up. Starcatherus pretends to consent, lets him come close and shatters his head (ibid.).

The difficulty begins with the second, and decisive, encounter. A young man, Hatherus, who is not introduced to us in advance, is returning from the hunt with his dogs and sees the scene from a distance. He does not recognize the old hero, and for sport or ridicule, sends toward him at a gallop two of his companions, who are of course received with blows of the crutches and killed. He himself approaches, recognizes Starcatherus without being recognized in turn, and asks whether he wishes to exchange one of his swords for a wagon, *an gladium vehiculo permutare vellet*. Moreover, nothing in his attitude is menacing or even insolent; a wagon would certainly be of more use to a cripple than would a second sword (ibid). But Starcatherus takes him for an *irrisor* and recites fifty-eight hexameters (p. 248) in which he laments the miseries of advanced age, of *senium*, and recalls his martial career and his past exploits (ll. 40–58; *at mihi si recolo, nascenti fata dedere / bella sequi, belloque mori* . . .). In the gap between these two themes (ll. 27–39) he expresses a remarkable wish, which suddenly places his young partner Hatherus in an unexpected light:

> . . . No one takes care of me, no soldier
> brings comfort to a veteran, unless Hatherus is here
> to help his shattered friend. Once he honors

anyone with his dutiful affection, true
from the start he attends him with the same unflagging
warmth, dreading to snap their initial bonds.
Frequently he bestows fitting rewards on war
heroes, venerates their spirit, grants his esteem
to the valiant and reveres famous comrades with gifts.
He scatters riches, strives to amass glowing
renown by his bounty and surpass many of the mighty.
Nor does his strength for the fight fall below his sense
of duty; quick to take arms, slow to waver,
ready to start the fray, yet ignorant how to
turn his back on a pressing foe.

Such then is the true nature of this carefree young hunter whom chance, apparently at least, has put before the old hero, who in his humiliation wished fervently to find him alone of all men for an assist which he does not specify. And the praise which he makes of him as an illustrious person would be fitting for the greatest Viking chiefs, as magnanimous toward their companions as they are courageous in the face of the enemy.

But at this point other poems inserted in the prose take us back again, recreating in verse the scene which has just been recounted to us in prose (p. 249). Hatherus makes his offer in twenty-two hexameters: that the old man sell him one of his swords for a wagon. In sixty-five hexameters, Starcatherus expresses his indignation to the stranger:

improbe, verba seris facili temeraria labio
auribus inconcinna piis. . . .

villain, your lips are glib in sowing rash talk,
inharmonious to a good man's ear. . . .

and recapitulates in detail the events of his glorious life.

Finally, there comes a dramatic surprise. From the turn which the conversation has taken the old man realizes that he has before him Hatherus. But, at the same stroke, we learn an astonishing fact: this Hatherus whom Starcatherus has longed for, counting on the faithfulness of his affection, is none other than the son of Lennus (or Lenno), one of the conspirators who had bribed him into killing Olo, and whom he had slain when he came back to his senses. Right away he sees in Hatherus the ideal executioner, the one he has been searching for, and he entreats him to kill him: is he not a youth of noble birth? Having a father to be avenged, does not this service which is asked of him match his own duty? Here is the scene until its conclusion (pp. 251–252):

> Thus Starcatherus. At last, in talking with him (*mutuo sermone*), he became aware that Hatherus was Lennus' son and realized the young man came of a distinguished family (*animadvertens iuvenem splendido loco natum*); he offered him his throat to cut, urging him not to shrink from taking satisfaction for his father's murder. He promised that if Hatherus complied, he would become possessor of that gold which Starcatherus had received from Lennus. To goad Hatherus into a fiercer mood toward him (*et ut eiusdem in se vehementius animum efferaret*), he is said to have egged him on like this:
>
> "Again, Hatherus, I bereaved you of Lenno, your father;
> pay me back, I beg, strike down an old man
> who longs to die, seek my gullet with avenging
> steel. For my spirit wishes this service from a noble
> headsman, but shudders to demand its doom from the right
> hand of a coward. A man may righteously choose
> to anticipate Destiny's law; what you cannot
> flee, you may even take in advance. A young
> tree must be nourished, an ancient one hewn down.
> Whoever overthrows what is close to its fate and fells
> what cannot stand is an instrument of Nature
> (*minister naturae est, quisquis fato confinia fundit. . .*).
> Death comes best when craved, life becomes tedious
> when the end is desired; do not let disagreeable
> age prolong an insupportable existence."

This sixth-century bronze die, one of four found at Torslunda (island of Öland) in Sweden, was used to make helmet plates. It depicts a young Odinic warrior in the presence of a berserk, not inappropriately for the Hatherus-Starcatherus encounter.

With these words he drew out his purse and proffered the money. Hatherus, excited by a passion to enjoy the fee no less than take revenge for his father, promised he would not spurn the payment but carry out his wishes. Starcatherus willingly offered him his sword and then bent forward his head beneath it; he urged Hatherus not to fulfil his task of executioner squeamishly or handle the blade like a girl, and told him that if, when he had killed him but before the body dropped, he could leap between the torso and its fallen head, he would be rendered proof against any weapon. It is uncertain whether he said this to instruct his murderer or to punish him (*quod utrum instruendi percussoris gratia an puniendi dixerit, incertum est*). Possibly the uncommon bulk of Starcatherus' body might have overwhelmed him as he sprang. Hatherus, then, drove his sword vigorously and lopped off the old man's head. The story tells how, severed from the trunk, it snapped at the soil with its teeth as it hit the ground, the fury of the dying jaws indicating his savage temper. Afraid that there could be treachery underlying the promise, his slayer prudently refrained from leaping, for if he had thoughtlessly done so, he might have been crushed under the impact of the descending body and paid for the old man's murder with his own life.

Hatherus burned the body on the field of Røling and had the ashes buried.

6. HÖÐR

This ending leaves the reader unsatisfied. To begin with there is the diversity, the contradictions in characters successively attributed to Hatherus. To the one which we have already taken up—the transformation of the young jokester into a renowned warlord, magnanimous and fearsome, who on top of this turns out to be the son of Lennus—yet another needs to be added. If Starcatherus, with all his last strength, desires his presence as that of the only friend who can help him in his despair, if he then recognizes in him the ideal executioner he seeks, it is because he admires and loves him, and this excludes any baseness or venality in the young man, crimes which the old hero has himself committed but once in his life, through fate, and for which he does not forgive himself. And yet he corrupts, as much as he depends upon, this beloved and admired youth. To the noble motives—to render a heroic service to an old man who requests it, and to avenge his father's blood—he adds an appeal to greed, the offer of the gold pieces that he carries about his neck. And the worst of it is that the young man appears amenable to this proposition. All of this, from the point of view of Germanic warrior morality, is of a mediocrity which it is hard to attribute to the original used by Saxo. There is moreover a more objective reason to see here an adulteration, a debasement. This contemptible motif is found only in the prose, whereas the brief poem, which is the last that Starcatherus will recite, and, like all those of the first books of the *Gesta Danorum* (of which it is also, absolutely, the last) is certainly an adaptation of native stanzas, makes no allusion to it, limiting itself to noble exhortations and no less noble generalities.

The reader's uneasiness has another cause, namely the uncertainty with which Saxo leaves him about the true last intentions of Starcatherus with regard to Hatherus, and, through this uncertainty, the author's insinuated preference for the most unpleasant alternative. Throughout his life, save for the three *facinora* imposed by Odin, our hero is a model not only of strength and courage, but of integrity and reliability. From his giant ancestry he carries certain physical traits, but his soul, apart perhaps from the harshness and intensity of his wrath, owes nothing to it; there is no trace of the excesses, the unbridled desires, the braggadocio, or the deceptions that characterize the normal behavior of giants. How is one to think that, at this last moment of his life, a deeper nature should take its revenge on him, and that he should with a villainous lie betray the youth who is only obeying him and only kills him in order to serve him? This would be a fourth *facinus*, a supernumerary one, that would destroy the sense and the structure of this long biography. Furthermore, the fear which Saxo ascribes to Hatherus is not justified by the outcome: the trunk and head do not clash like the Symplegades, and if the dying head carries on ferociously on the ground, it has no thought for the man who has severed it. Thus the situation is quite different from others with which one might at first be tempted to compare it, for example the scene which the Caucasian legends of Soslan-Sosryko describe in numerous variants.[21] There the hero has managed with difficulty to defeat a specific enemy, a giant, as stupid as he is strong; reduced to power-

[21] See my *Légendes sur les Nartes* (1930), no. 21, pp. 77–83 (six variants); *Le Livre des héros*, pp. 89–94.

lessness, trapped and unable to escape death, the giant feigns a sudden benevolence: after having beheaded him, he says, his captor should draw out of his neck a particular tendon and make a belt of it; thus he will inherit some of his strength. Justifiably suspicious, Sosryko tries out the belt on a tree, which breaks or crumbles, burned to ashes. In other versions, once the giant is decapitated, his head leaps toward Sosryko and seizes the sword tight in its jaws. Sosryko begins to run but the head does not let go; finally, though, it slackens its hold, falls, and Sosryko is able to scalp it. In this case, and in all the analogous cases, the giant or monster is faithful to his nature, prolonging at the moment of his death a hostility and treachery that have never been contradicted or concealed. The circumstances of Starcatherus' death are entirely otherwise, and one has the impression that Saxo has gone wrong in not choosing the "better" interpretation, in not admitting that his hero is sincere and simply reducing the scene to this commonplace theme of the giant wreaking posthumous vengeance.[22] Starcatherus has before him a man whom he admires, respects, loves; he asks of him an exceptional service which will be in no way a fault, nor require any vengeance. He gives him at the outset (with a disagreeable touch of venality) all that he possesses materially, but he wishes also to bequeath to him a more valuable treasure, not the strength that he carries within him, but the compounded sum of this strength which he himself has not drawn on, namely invulnerability. This he can only do by a sort of crossing of their bodies, an insertion of the youth's entire body between the still-twitching fragments of his own, at the very moment when there would pass, from head to trunk or from trunk to head, the last mysterious current of his life force: a gift and also a fusing, a union.

But who exactly is Hatherus, this figure whom we have already seen to be incoherent even more than complex? It has long been

[22] And to another magical theme: the efficacy of passing between the severed parts of a corpse (purification; acquiring of privileges); see Olivier Masson, "A propos d'un rituel hittite pour la lustration d'une armée: le rite de purification par le passage entre les deux parties d'une victime," *Revue de l'histoire des religions,* CXXXVII (1950), 1–25.

thought that Saxo, by misunderstanding or design, has here debased and humanized a divine figure, namely Höðr, the son of Odin. In the mythology which survives, Höðr only appears as the blind, unwitting killer of Baldr, and after the destruction and restoration of the world, in association with Baldr as Odin's successor. But there are reasons—Höðr continues an ancient Indo-European warrior name[23]—to think that he was originally a more general figure of Fate, in particular the fate of the fighter, with its long uncertainty and its more than probable outcome.[24] The phonetic difficulty —*Hatherus* transcribes **Haðr* rather than *Höðr*—does not seem insoluble; the second element of the compound *Stark-(h)aðr*[25] may have affected the vowel color of the uncompounded **Hotherus*, and this is all the more likely as it is plausible that, having elsewhere used Höðr-Hotherus (Høtherus[26]) with his correct name form in reducing him to a human figure, and no longer understanding the theology of the god Höðr, Saxo preferred not to repeat the same name exactly.

Further efforts have occasionally been made in this direction, for example by the late Jan de Vries in his (1955) article on Starkaðr.[27] According to him, here as elsewhere in the myth of Baldr, Höðr did not have his own separate existence but was simply "eine Erscheinungsform des Gottes Oðinn," a manifestation of the god

[23] Jan de Vries, *Altnordisches etymologisches Wörterbuch* (1961), pp. 278–279: OIce. *höð* 'battle,' OHG *hadu*, OE *heaðu*: OIrish *cath* 'battle' (Gaulish *Caturiges*), Thracian Κατυ-, etc.

[24] *Gods of the Ancient Northmen* (Berkeley, Los Angeles, London 1973), chap. 3 ("The Drama of the World: Balder, Hoder, Loki"); *ME I* (1968), pp. 222–230.

[25] Jan de Vries, op. cit., p. 544, s.v. "*starkr*", writes: "Dazu PN. *Starkaðr* ält. *Störkuðr* (< *Stark-höðr*), vgl. ogot. *Starcedius* (= *Starki-þius* . . .), fränk. *Starchildis, Starkfrid*, ae. *Starkwulf*, langob. *Starcolf*." As the second term in compounds, **haðuR* gives sometimes *-(h)uðr* (*Niðuðr* 'der grimmige Krieger' = OHG *Nīdhad*, OE *Niðhad; Dörruðr* 'der Speerkämpfer'), sometimes *-(h)aðr* (*Andaðr* 'der Gegner', **Anda-haðuR* beside *Anduðr, Önduðr*). Cf. Birger Nerman, *Studier över Svärges hedna Litteratur* (1913), pp. 108–109.

[26] See "Høtherus et Balderus," *Beiträge zur Geschichte der deutschen Sprache und Literatur*, 83 (1962), pp. 259–270: reprinted as Appendix 3 in *From Myth to Fiction* (Chicago, 1973).

[27] Cited above, p. 11; the text quoted here is on p. 296.

Odin, and the very name of Starkaðr made of this character "ein Prototyp der odinischen Weihenkrieger," emphasizing "den religiösen Charakter dieser Vorstellung." For my part I am not inclined to accept this reduction of multiple gods to one; the procedure has done much harm in the study, for example, of Roman religion, where goddesses as different as Mater Matuta, Feronia, Carna, and so on have been considered as so many specific "numina" of one vast Juno. It is no more to be recommended for the interpretation of Scandinavian religion. Höðr is one of the figures in the orbit of the sovereign-magical-warrior god Odin, and one of those closest to him, to be sure, but he remains distinct, and I am not resigned to admitting that Odin, in the myth of Baldr, openly, under his own name, should at first try to prevent and in the end lament a murder which he has meanwhile committed under cover of another name. With this reservation, maintaining the duality of Höðr and Odin, I think nonetheless that Jan de Vries is correct when he writes, after having mentioned the murderer of Baldr:

> There is yet a second Höðr: the Hatherus who appears in the account of the death of Starkaðr. He is the son of the Dane Lenno, whom Starkaðr has killed, and he is bound to Starkaðr by a loyal friendship; yet it is he who gives him *den heissersehnten Todesstreich*. According to Schneider, Hatherus is a late, in no way heroic figure. This is by no means so; it is Odin himself, the divine Höðr, who recalls Starkaðr to him at the end of his life (*Starkaðr zu sich heimholt*). One should take note of the singular form of the killing: there is no combat; on the contrary the decrepit old man extends his head to the youth, as a sacrificial victim, *pronam cervicem applicuit*, and Hatherus has only to strike. . . .

Following the text more closely, we would say: at the point when two of the *facinora* of Starcatherus imposed by Odin (in Saxo) or by Thor (in the *Gautrekssaga*) have already been committed and the third *facinus* is in the making, Hatherus, that is to say the god Höðr, Fate, close to Odin, strikes up a friendly relationship with the old Starcatherus in the guise of a young man, as (in the *Gautrekssaga*) Odin himself of old, in the appearance of the mature man Hrosshársgrani, became the tutor of the young Starkaðr in view of obtaining from him, after years of care, the first *facinus*. Once the third *facinus* is accomplished, and with it the last extension of his life is exhausted, Starcatherus, suddenly deteriorated and wishing to die, calls in his prayers for the presence of this Höðr, whom he finds, providentially rather than by chance, and has himself killed by him once he has recognized him. Finally, at the moment when he is to die, he wishes at least to transfer to his killer the privilege of invulnerability which he himself has possessed only latently. In the reality of theology, this would be literally a transfusion of the hero into the god, but under human guise it is no more than a gift which the old man offers the young. And of course in the novelistic account, the human form carries the day: cut off from his origin and his theological value, Hatherus is only a human individual who hesitates, is suspicious of the gift, and finally does not receive it.

Having at our disposal only Saxo's awkward and inaccurate adaptation, it is impossible to be more affirmative or more precise regarding this conclusion. What is essential is as follows:

Our hero—this six-armed giant reduced by amputation to human shape, or this grandson of an eight-armed giant, human but marked with inherited scars—after having been in his youth the object, the pawn of the opposing attentions of the gods Thor and Odin, and after developing his career within the framework of three lives granted and three *facinora* imposed by one or the other of the gods, voluntarily ends his life and career by having himself slain by a young man behind whom we glimpse a third god, very close to Odin, Höðr. To this young man he declares his affection and wishes, no doubt sincerely, to transfuse into him the best part of himself. The finale of the story, as we see, is no less strange than the beginning.

Now the Indic epic knows a hero of the same type, whom we shall follow, too, from a monstrous birth miraculously repaired to his decapitation and absorption by the god *percussor*.

II

ŚIŚUPĀLA

1. THE BIRTH AND DESTINY OF ŚIŚUPĀLA

Śiśupāla is, in the *Mahābhārata*, an incidental character.[1] Close kinship ties exist and hostile relations develop between him and Kṛṣṇa, but he has no blood relation nor alliance with the Pāṇḍavas, and does not have to intervene, on one side or the other, in the conflict in which all the great names of the epic confront each other; he is put to death beforehand in Book Two. Still, according to the rules of the game, this apparently wholly human being is the incarnation of a being from the beyond, the powerful demon who in several previous lives has already confronted other incarnations of Viṣṇu: Hiraṇyakaśipu, whom the god fought and slew in the guise of the man-lion; later Rāvaṇa, over whom Viṣṇu-Rāma prevailed with difficulty.[2] These antecedents barely enter into the plot of the poem, simply justifying that Śiśupāla should be by nature a determined adversary of Kṛṣṇa-Viṣṇu. But, in accord with

[1] The episode of Śiśupāla occupies ślokas 1307–1627 of the second book (*Sabhāparvan*) in the Calcutta edition (matching van Buitenen pp. 91–104). The late poem of Māgha has nothing to offer for our purposes; see *Bālamāgha, Māgha's Śiśupālavadha im Auszuge, bearbeitet von Carl Cappeller* (1915), and *Māgha's Śiśupālavadha, ins Deutsche übertragen von E. Hultzsch* (1926). For the Purāṇic accounts (particularly the *Bhāgavata Purāṇa*) see V. R. Ramachandra Dikshitar, *The Purāṇa Index*, III (1955), 423, s.v. "Śiśupāla."

[2] Edward W. Hopkins, *Epic Mythology* (1915), pp. 51, 211.

another rule of transposition, this deep causality is replicated on the earthly level by another, more immediate and more novelistic one.

Śiśupāla is introduced in the following way. After their childhood, and despite their already serious conflicts with their cousins, the hundred sons of Dhṛtarāṣṭra (and especially with the eldest, Duryodhana), the Pāṇḍavas have not as yet known their great misfortunes, as it is only at the end of Book Two, the *Sabhāparvan*, that Duryodhana's malice and Dhṛtarāṣṭra's weakness will arrange the fateful dice-game which, by fleecing Yudhiṣṭhira and his brothers and forcing them into thirteen years of exile, begins a conflict between the two groups of cousins that will be settled only in the bloody battle of the "field of the Kurus," *Kurukṣetra*, from Book Six to Book Ten. To all appearances, at the moment, things are on the way to turning out otherwise: Yudhiṣṭhira's rights to kingship seem to be recognized by everyone, including the blind uncle and the maniacal Duryodhana; he has received the first visit from his cousin Kṛṣṇa, who is none other than Viṣṇu incarnate (as Yudhiṣṭhira himself is either the son, or the incarnation of a portion of Dharma),[3] and Kṛṣṇa has begun the part which he will play throughout the poem, that of faithful, lucid, discreet and resourceful counsellor. Yudhiṣṭhira has been discussing with him the advisability of celebrating a *rājasūya*, the ceremony of royal consecration, or "sprinkling," here curiously conceived as an imperial ceremony, bestowing on the recipient not only royalty, *rāṣṭra*, but *sāmrājya*, "universal kingship" and *pārthivya*, "earthly sovereignty," implying in consequence recognition by all other kings of a more or less effective sort of supremacy.

[3] This phrase does not pretend to solve the large set of problems posed by the character of Kṛṣṇa in the *Mahābhārata*. My feeling is certainly that much of what is said of him is sufficiently explained as transposition of the mythology of an ancient Viṣṇu, a transposition of the same sort and scope as that which has produced the Pāṇḍavas from an archaic list of the functional gods. But of course, Kṛṣṇa is not only that. Here, it suffices that the equivalence Kṛṣṇa-Viṣṇu is explicitly stated in the course of the episode.

A first obstacle has already been averted, or rather eliminated. Another prince, Jarāsaṇdha the king of Magadha, had launched the same claim to sovereignty as Yudhiṣṭhira, and had begun to back it up with cruelty and indeed barbarity, backed by the support of the god Rudra-Śiva. In the presence of Kṛṣṇa, on his advice and almost on his orders, two of Yudhiṣṭhira's brothers have disposed of this competitor under dramatic circumstances which we will examine later.[4]

Yudhiṣṭhira has then dispatched his four younger brothers to the four corners of the world to secure, and if need be to compel, the consent of the kings. Without much trouble these missions have succeeded and the kings have poured into Yudhiṣṭhira's capital to attend the ceremony and thus to confirm their allegiance. The Pāṇḍavas have before them truly a gallery of kings, seemingly well disposed, among them Vasudeva, accompanied by his son Kṛṣṇa, that is to say again, Viṣṇu incarnate.

Things get off to a good start, with the usual ceremonies of hospitality, particularly the *arghya,* the offering presented to the guests of honor. But very quickly there arises a serious problem, an unexpected quarrel which remotely recalls the Irish legends, where the "hero's portion" regularly provokes competitions and battles. In this case it has to do not with such a portion, but with a supplementary *arghya,* an *arghya* of excellence, which Bhīṣma (the great-uncle, tutor, and counsellor of the whole family of the Bhāratas, the sons of Dhṛtarāṣṭra and those of Pāṇḍu alike) proposes to offer to the most worthy of those present (1330). Yudhiṣṭhira agrees and asks Bhīṣma himself to designate the one to be so honored. Bhīṣma does not hesitate and responds, with good reasons: Kṛṣṇa (1332–1334). The assembled kings would surely accede to this award without grumbling when one of them rises and protests vehemently; it is Śiśupāla, the king of Cedi. He refuses to accept that, in an assembly of kings, a special honor should go to an individual who is not a king.

[4] See below, chap. IV.

His protest rapidly occasions an ever more lively exchange of words and the old Bhīṣma, who has lived through three generations and harbors much knowledge, is led to explain to Bhīmasena, the second of the Pāṇḍavas who is not exactly well-informed and whom Śiśupāla has taken personally to task, who this spoilsport is, how he came into the world, what fate weighs upon him, and also why up to this moment Kṛṣṇa has shown so much patience towards him (1494–1522). The tale of his beginnings follows.

Śiśupāla was well-born in the royal family of the Cedis, the son of the reigning king. But he was born monstrous: he had three eyes and four arms (*tryakṣaḥ caturbhujaḥ*), and uttered inarticulate cries like an animal (1494). His distraught parents were all set to abandon him, *tyāgāya kurutām matim* (1495), when a disembodied voice, *vāg aśarīriṇī*, made itself heard to the king, his wife, and his assembled ministers. The voice said (1497–1498):

> "King, he is born your son, illustrious and powerful, therefore be not afraid of him, but guard your child anxiously. You are not to be his death, nor has this Time yet come. His death, his slayer by the sword, has been born, lord of men."

Hearing this speech which came from the invisible, *vākyam antarhitam*, the mother speaks, tormented by the affection she feels, in spite of everything, for this small monster, her son (*putrasnehābhisantaptā*) (1500–1501):

> "I bow with folded hands to him who has spoken this word concerning my son. Now let him also speak further. I want to hear who shall be the death of this son!"

Then the invisible being speaks again (1502–1503):

> "He upon whose lap his two extra arms will both fall on the ground like five-headed snakes and that third eye in the middle of the child's forehead will sink away as he looks at him—he shall be his death."

Thus the prophecy is twofold, but unambiguous: one day, placed in someone's lap, the monstrous child will lose his excesses, two arms and the central eye, and will become normal; but the Deliverer who will work this anatomical miracle will also later be the cause of his death.

Rumor of such a remarkable occurrence travels fast, and all the kings of the earth, drawn by curiosity, *didṛkṣavaḥ,* come to the country and the palace where it took place. The king of Cedi receives them all with honor and places his baby upon the lap of each, *ekaikasya nṛpasyāṅke putram aropayat tadā,* and on the knees of every single one, *pṛthak,* of these thousands of kings, *rājasahasrāṇām,* but the spectacle, the expected miracle never occurs, *śiśur aṅke samārūḍho na tat prāpa nidarśanam.*

So it goes until there arrive from the town of Dvāravatī, attracted by the reports, two princes, who have moreover excellent reasons for coming, since the small monster's mother is their paternal aunt. These two princes are the Yādavas Kṛṣṇa and his older brother Balarāma. They too are received with honor, and the queen personally has just placed her son on Kṛṣṇa's knees, *putram dāmoda-rotsaṅge devī saṃvyadadhāt svayam* (1510). Then finally, the miracle occurs (1511):

> ". . . No sooner was he placed on his lap than the two extra arms fell off and the eye in his forehead sank away."

Seeing this, the mother is troubled and begins to tremble (*vyathitā, trastā*), and understandably: according to the disembodied Voice, the man whose touch has worked this transformation will also be the *mṛtyu,* the (cause of) death of the small being restored to human form. She asks a favor of her nephew (1512 –1513):

> "Give a boon to me, Kṛṣṇa, who am sick with fear, strongarmed one, for you are the relief of the oppressed and grant safety to those that are afeared!"

Kṛṣṇa answers (1514–1515):

> "Do not fear. . . . What boon must I give you, or what should I do, my aunt? Whether it can be done or not, I shall obey your word!"

Then the queen makes her appeal (1516):

> "Pray pardon, strong man, the derelictions of Śiśupāla!"

Kṛṣṇa answers (1517):

> "I shall forsooth forgive a hundred derelictions of your son, paternal aunt, even though they may be capital offenses. Do not sorrow."

Thus the fate of Śiśupāla was sealed. We shall soon learn that the account of these hundred offenses, the *aparādhāḥ* to be tolerated, is exhausted and even overdrawn. Released from the promise to his aunt, Kṛṣṇa will in the end be able to punish Śiśupāla.

2. RUDRA, KṚṢṆA AND ŚIŚUPĀLA

Before proceeding further, let us ponder this monstrous birth, this correction of shape and this boon linking *facinora* and longevity.

India is more familiar than Scandinavia with persons with extra arms, not only among babies, but adults as well, including the greatest of them—*caturbhuja* 'four-armed' is a frequent Hindu epithet of Viṣṇu as well as of Śiva, and there come immediately to mind the figures of Indian gods who seem to have more arms, all gracefully and symmetrically arrayed, than the Hydra of Lerna had heads. The *Mahābhārata* mentions other births of children, even quite human ones, with several arms, which occasion no such alarm nor grief. Here, the fear is immediate: the father and mother can think only of abandoning the infant, and would do so if the Voice of an unseen being did not intervene. We are faced with a peculiar case.

But this is not what is most important. Long ago it was noted that the second congenital deformity of the "little one," the third eye in the middle of his forehead, *lalāṭajaṃ nayanam,* clearly marks him as a human replica of Rudra-Śiva. It is this god, and he alone—and very early, if the epithet *tryambaka* means, at least by connotation, "having three pupils"—who enjoys the privilege of having three eyes, the third between the two normal ones in the middle of the forehead: *tricakṣus, tryakṣa* are epithets of Śiva.[5]

Along the same line it has been pointed out that the name of Śiśupāla, for which the *Mahābhārata* (1497) suggests an obviously postfabricated etymology,[6] is a transposition, to the level of the "small" (*śiśu-*), of the already Vedic epithet of Rudra, and frequently later of Rudra-Śiva, *paśupati; paśupati* is "lord of animals"; *śiśupāla* is "protector (and also "king, prince") of the small."

Finally, in a previous episode—which he himself recalls within the present one—Śiśupāla manifests a particular attachment, to the extent of being his "army chief," to King Jarāsandha, who will occupy us later and who is presented as the favorite of Rudra-Śiva, endowed with the privilege of seeing Rudra-Śiva with his own eyes, and who offers kings in sacrifice to Rudra-Śiva.[7]

These reasons oblige us to conclude, as did John Muir more than a century ago (1864),[8] that Śiśupāla is, as solidly by nature as he is ephemerally in form, a hero "on the side of Rudra-Śiva," a transformation of this Rudra-Śiva whose own incarnation is another of the poem's fearsome heroes, Aśvatthāman.[9]

And this is of great interest because the one who delivers him from his superfluous arms and eye, and with whom he will nonetheless remain to the end in a state of violent hostility, is Kṛṣṇa-Viṣṇu, a god of a completely different sort. In more than one regard the "opposite" of Rudra-Śiva, he will even be, in the Hindu trinity, his polar partner. Śiśupāla is thus found, from his earliest youth, in contradictory relationships with the two great gods.

[5] Edward W. Hopkins, *Epic Mythology*, pp. 220, 221.
[6] Śl. 1497 (van Buitenen p. 100).
[7] See below, chap. IV.
[8] *Original Sanskrit Texts*, IV, 170–180.
[9] *ME I*, pp. 213–222.

At the same time that, miraculously, by the mere touch of Kṛṣṇa-Viṣṇu, he is restored to human shape, Śiśupāla receives from the same Kṛṣṇa a true "fate," which by defining a postponement completes what the unknown Voice had imposed on him at birth. The Voice had said that death would come to him from his very normalizer, to be precise, that his normalizer "would be his death." When it is discovered that the normalizer is Kṛṣṇa-Viṣṇu, the latter undertakes to delay this death. He does not define the reprieve in terms of absolute or lived time, he does not say, for example, "a hundred years" or "three average human lives"; rather he sets down a kind of sliding scale which ties the young being's life span to his behavior: "I will tolerate, without killing him, a hundred offenses, *aparādhaśatam*, any of which would deserve death." This number can reassure the mother; even between people who hate each other, to commit a hundred offenses each of which merits death requires a certain amount of time, and especially since the interested party will be forewarned, it will be up to him not to exhaust his credit and to avoid overstepping the limit by a hundred and first offense. In fact it comes out in the episode of Book Two that Śiśupāla has wasted no time; he has carried on like a prodigal son, squandering his store of impunity, and he is still young when here, before us, he overdraws his account, by an offense which will bring on his death. It is no less remarkable that the boon granted him concerning the length of his life should be limited and conditioned by a counting of *aparādhāḥ*, that is, of *facinora* committed against someone.

A final remark will serve to tie together the two preceding statements. It is at the mother's request that Kṛṣṇa grants this gift to the baby, and by asking for it moreover in a very general way (to tolerate his offenses, without specifying a number) she shows that she has no doubt of the enmity that will prevail between normalizer and normalizee, the latter's agressiveness being exerted consistently at the expense of the former. Has she recognized Rudra-Śiva in the one as she knows that the other is Viṣṇu? In any case, one could not wish for a better expression of the "conflict of divinities" which, from the foreordained immunity until the hundredth offense, will dominate the career of Śiśupāla.

3. THE OFFENSES

Let us return to the biography of the hero. The texts are not prolix either about his exploits or his crimes: undoubtedly they were the subject of specific, well-known tales, and only allusions are made to them here. The exploits of Śiśupāla must have been numerous, since he commanded the armies of another king of whom it is said expressly that he had conquered a large part of the world (574):

> The mighty king Śiśupāla, having indeed gone over competely to this Jarāsandha's side, has become his marshal (*senāpatiḥ*).

Regarding the hundred personal affronts deserving of death, *vadhārha* (1517), which Kṛṣṇa has undertaken to forgive, we do not have the complete list either. At the moment of the final settling of accounts, Kṛṣṇa gives merely a sampling of them, recalling only five, in five *ślokas*. All have been committed against members of Kṛṣṇa's family, the Yādavas, but in view of familial solidarity they ought to be considered as in effect directed against him and consequently charged to the current account of patience on which the offender keeps drawing (1516). What are these examples (1566–1572)?

> 1. "Knowing that we had gone to the city of Prāgjyotiṣa, this fiend, who is our cousin, burned down Dvārakā [= Dvāravatī, our capital], kings."
> 2. "While the barons of the Bhojas were at play on Mount Raivataka, he slew and captured them, then returned to his city."
> 3. "Malevolently, he stole the horse that was set free at the Horse Sacrifice and surrounded by guards to disrupt my father's sacrifice."
> 4. "When she was journeying to the country of the Sauvīras to be given in marriage, the misguided fool abducted the unwilling wife-to-be of the glorious Babhru."
> 5. "Hiding beneath his wizardry, the fiendish offender of his uncle abducted Bhadrā of Viśāla, the intended bride of the Karūṣa!
>
> For the sake of my father's sister I have endured very great suffering; but fortunately now *this* is taking place in the

presence of all the kings. For you are now witnesses of the all-surpassing offense against me; learn also now the offenses he has perpetrated against me in concealment."

It is easy to verify that these sample offenses are distributed, in the order II (first and second offenses), I (third offense), and III (fourth and fifth offenses), across the framework of the three functions, and constitute a new example of the theme of the "three sins of the warrior":

In 1 and 2, Śiśupāla, instead of fairly and openly giving battle, waits until he knows a king is absent to burn down his capital, and surprises *rājanyas* in the midst of disporting themselves to massacre or kidnap them: this cowardice is on the same level as that of the second sin of Indra and Herakles slaying an adversary by a foul trick, instead of confronting him in equal combat.

In 3, Śiśupāla attacks the king in the area of religion by preventing him from celebrating the most solemn of royal sacrifices.

In 4 and 5, Śiśupāla abducts a noble married woman—in 5, disguising himself as her husband—committing a sexual sin entirely similar to the third sin of Indra, and as serious as the third sin of Herakles.

The great similarity of the two first and the two last offenses makes it probable that this list has been inflated—India has little taste for conciseness—and that more originally each type of sin was illustrated by only one example. Taking this tack, it is tempting to suppose also that the number "one hundred" has been substituted, for the same reason, for the simple number "three," and that what is presented here as a sampling of the offenses—or rather what this sampling was before the development of the three crimes into five—originally constituted their complete inventory.

In any case, directly or indirectly, all these sins are directed against the king. The first three, those of the second and first function, are direct, attacking the king in his capital, his servants, his religion; the two sexual sins attack women belonging to the king's family or placed under his protection. Rhetorically speaking, therefore, in this final quarrel where Śiśupāla claims to defend royal majesty and where he tries, we shall see, to incite the assembly of kings against Kṛṣṇa and the Pāṇḍavas, this enumeration of crimes committed against a king, in the three functional areas of royal activity, is very timely, and will in the end have on the audience the effect which Kṛṣṇa is hoping for.

4. ŚIŚUPĀLA AND THE KINGS

The dispute during which at first Bhīṣma, then Kṛṣṇa himself, reveal the past and unveil the nature of their adversary, develops at length and occasions several speeches by Śiśupāla. While they do not become more and more violent, for the first is already extremely so, they rather lead gradually up to the desperate defiance at the end. Their subject is, from beginning to end, the defense of the majesty of kings, purported to have been violated because the supplementary *arghya* has been accorded not to one of them, but to Kṛṣṇa, who is no king: Śiśupāla makes himself the champion of this outraged assembly.

The theme is stated from the outset (1338), when Bhīṣma hears him say:

> "This Vārṣṇeya does not deserve regal honor as though he were a king, Kauravya, while great-spirited lords of the earth are present!"

It is on *dharma* that he bases himself, he says quickly, in a haughty, didactic tone, to the Pāṇḍavas who are astounded at this effrontery (1340):

> "You are children, you don't know! For the Law is subtle, Pāṇḍavas!"

And the flood is loosed (1342):

> "How can the Dāśārha, who is no king, merit precedence over all the kings of the earth so that he should be honored by you?"

Growing angrier, he lists the kings and other heroes who are present, and praises their virtues—beginning with this very Bhīṣma whom he attacks as if guilty of lese majesty; how, he asks, can they distinguish and honor Kṛṣṇa when there are present Aśvatthāman, Duryodhana, Kṛpa, Druma, Karṇa, and many others (1347–1353)?

> "If you must honor Madhusūdana, why bring these kings here—to insult them, Bhārata?
>
> It was not out of fear for the great-spirited Kaunteya that we all offered him tribute, nor out of greed or to flatter him. He wanted the sovereignty and proceeded according to Law; so we gave him tribute and now he does not count us! What but contempt moves you, if in an assembly of kings you honor Kṛṣṇa with the guest gift, while he has not attained to the title? . . . Not only is there delivered an insult to these Indras of kings, the Kurus have also shown you up for what you obviously are, Janārdana. As a marriage is to a eunuch, as a show is to a blind man, so is this royal honor to you Madhusūdana, who are no king!"

The exposition is instructive by its very monotony: it reveals a dominating concept of the thought and ideology of Śiśupāla.

Bhīṣma's reply is grandiose. He rejects, without deigning to discuss it, this limited conception of *dharma,* opposing to it the greater truth: Kṛṣṇa is indeed more than a king, he is everything, he has everything:

> "It is in the full knowledge of his fame, his bravery, and his triumph that we offer the honor. . . . Of brahmins he is the elder in knowledge, of barons the superior in strength, and both these grounds to honor Govinda are found firm. Knowledge of the Vedas and their branches, and boundless might as well—who in the world of men possesses these so distinguishedly if not Keśava?"[10]

[10] Śl. 1384–1387 (van Buitenen p. 95). The Poona edition, which is quoted here in translation, rightly omits the first line, which introduces the *vaiśyas* and *śūdras* into the matter.

But Śiśupāla does not relent, and the assembly of the kings begins to react. For all of Bhīṣma's saying, "Look at these many kings older than you are: they consent to the honor paid Kṛṣṇa, and you should likewise forbear it" (1372), the audience is becoming more and more susceptible to this royalist demagogy which Śiśupāla pours forth in eloquent torrents. Sahadeva, the youngest of the Pāṇḍavas, is soon obliged to threaten to put his foot on the head of anyone who would challenge the decision, and at the sight of his foot none of the kings dares utter a word (1402–1405). But when Śiśupāla leaves the hall, they all follow him, and their wrath is great. One of them, Sunītha, incites them to attack those who have tried to humiliate them, and they make ready to prevent the sacrifice, *yajñopaghātāya* (1410–1412), so that, says the poet, "When they were being restrained by their friends, their appearance was like that of roaring lions that are dragged away from their raw meat. Kṛṣṇa then understood that the invincible sea of kings, surrounded by billowing troops, was making a covenant for war."

Things do not come to such a pass, however, and Bhīṣma, the Nestor of this epic, has good reason to say "Let these kings bark like a pack of dogs around a sleeping lion. . . ." And he hints at something quite interesting, which will lead us quickly towards the end, the death of Śiśupāla: this fine devotion to kings, this intransigence about the rights of kings, are they genuine? No, says Bhīṣma, repeating the image of dogs; Kṛṣṇa is for the moment like a sleeping lion, and before he wakes, the king of Cedi makes lions out of all these dogs. But in reality, unconsciously (*acetanaḥ*, 1427),

> ". . . he desires with all his being to lead them all to the abode of Yama. . . !"

And this accusation, which matches one of the well-known cruelties of Jarāsandha, the king whom Śiśupāla has served as commander-in-chief, must have substance, for Śiśupāla protests vigorously (1433):

> "How is it you are not ashamed of yourself, decrepit defiler of your family, while you frighten all these kings with your many threats?"

In the last speech which he will give, in the face of the fate that awaits him, he will take up again the theme of offended royal dignity, and after another catalogue of kings who deserve to be honored, he will conclude by repeating the theme in the interrogative (1540–1541): "Why," he will say to Bhīṣma,

> "Why do you fail to praise such kings as Śalya and others, if as always your heart is set on praising, Bhīṣma?"

In the moments preceding the death of this overreacher, there occurs in the kings a change, a reversal. Kṛṣṇa has presented his grievances, has recalled the hundred offenses of which he has given five examples and which are affronts to the majesty and status of a king, and has called them all to witness the hundred and first which has been committed against him. The outcome is this (1575):

> All the assembled kings, upon hearing this and more from Vāsudeva, now began to revile the Cedi king.

In fact they watch without serious reaction the execution of Śiśupāla—and we shall see presently the remarkable mode of this death. Immediately after, when the body has been removed, Yudhiṣṭhira celebrates his *rājasūya* before the assembly of kings, as if no incident had marred the festivities. In the end, he dismisses his guests, including Kṛṣṇa, with honor, setting down the official version in his final proclamation (1604): "All these kings have come to us in a spirit of friendship."

Thus, in short, the rights of kings have been the subject of Śiśupāla's protest; afterwards the kings themselves, their loyalty and their choice have been at stake in the rhetorical debate; and finally, after coming close to an ill-timed insurrection, the kings have done what was expected of them, that for which they had been invited: their consenting presence has fully validated the rite.

5. THE END OF ŚIŚUPĀLA; ŚIŚUPĀLA AND KṚṢṆA

We left Kṛṣṇa and Śiśupāla, incarnate Viṣṇu and the "little Śiva," at the moment when Kṛṣṇa announces that the present offense, the hundred and first, is no longer covered by his promise of forbearance and will not be tolerated. Śiśupāla replies (1579):

> "Forgive me, if you have that much faith, or don't, Kṛṣṇa, what could possibly befall me from you, however angry or friendly?"

Defiance of the Commander? Resignation to fate? The end of a good loser? In any case, from this moment on, Kṛṣṇa's mind is made up. According to the Calcutta edition, he "thinks" of the *cakra* (*manasā 'cintayac cakram*), the discus, his infallible weapon that has already punished the excesses of so many demons. The discus right away appears and positions itself in his hand. At this solemn moment Kṛṣṇa explains the situation once more, justifying his action. Then he acts (1582–1589):[11]

> ["Let the kings hear why I have put up with this: I have had to forgive a hundred of his offenses, at his mother's request. What she asked of me, I have given, and the tally is complete. Now I shall slay him before the eyes of all you earthlords." So saying, at that moment the best of the Yadus,] scourge of his enemies, irately cut off his head with his discus. The strong-armed king fell like a tree that is struck by a thunderbolt.
>
> Thereupon the kings watched a sublime radiance rise forth from the body of the king of the Cedis, which, great king, was like the sun rising up from the sky; and that radiance greeted lotus-eyed Kṛṣṇa, honored by the world, and entered him, O king. When they saw that, all the kings deemed it a miracle that that radiance entered the strong-armed man, that greatest of men. In a cloudless sky heaven rained forth and blazing lightning struck and the earth trembled, when Kṛṣṇa

[11] The Poona edition rejects the end of Kṛṣṇa's speech and the following line.

slew the Caidya. There were kings there who did not say a word. . . .[12]

Thus, at the moment of the death of this madman who has never ceased, throughout his life, to pile up offenses and crimes against Kṛṣṇa, and who has just showered him once again with insolence, the best part of himself, his *tejaḥ agryam*, leaves his beheaded body in the form of a brilliant light and enters into his executioner, merging with him. It is indeed a miraculous spectacle, *adbhutam*, as the kings who are present all agree.

How is this miracle to be explained? The editors of the *Mahābhārata* see no difficulty here: Kṛṣṇa-Viṣṇu is the god who encompasses all, of whom all beings, despite appearances, are parts. His enemy Śiśupāla was therefore, in spite of himself, a part of this total Being. The total being has simply wished to recover the part, and one may suppose that he has attracted him by some sort of hypnosis. Just before entering into the body of his killer, it seems that Śiśupāla has understood the meaning of the act: his *tejas* salutes the god, *vavande tat tadā tejo viveśa ca*. But until then he had not been in on the secret. During the final quarrel, he has been seized by a kind of intoxication, an irresistible need to reenter the womb of the incarnate All, a surprising variation on the maternal womb of the psychoanalysts. Consciously, he has rushed to his destruction, has provoked it, discarding all recourse. Unconsciously, it was something else: he was obeying the call, the will of Kṛṣṇa-Viṣṇu. Bhīṣma, the wise and experienced old man, had made a correct diagnosis when, some pages earlier, he ended his account of the birth and childhood of Śiśupāla with these words, which attempted to explain to the Pāṇḍavas the paroxysm of violence to which the challenger abandoned himself (1521–1522):

> "He of a certainty is a particle of the glory of Hari, strong-armed prince, and widely famous Hari wants to recover it.

[12] Some of the kings to be sure, the text goes on (1590–1591), do indeed show their anger, wringing their hands and biting their lips, but they do not act, approval prevails and everything soon quiets down.

That is why this evil-minded king of Cedis roars fiercely like a tiger, tiger of the Kurus, without worrying about any of us."

This is in fact why he plunges into the hundred and first misdeed, which he could easily have avoided or held back. At the very time when he cries out his indifference to what Kṛṣṇa will or will not do—these, as we saw, are his last words—he is possessed by an unconscious need to make an end of it, to lose himself in the being whom he insults.

The Greek tragedians did not have to deal with this type of drama, but it is on a par with the loftiest situations which they encountered: Prometheus standing up to Zeus, Oedipus obstinately delving into his destiny. Śiśupāla is not a normal man; only thanks to Kṛṣṇa, to Viṣṇu, has he been freed from the bodily monstrosity that revealed him as a little Śiva. But, from the instant of this boon, the child's mother and Kṛṣṇa himself have foreseen the future: from this humanized Śiva to Viṣṇu incarnate, there will be, by an irresistible bent of nature—one might readily say, of theology—nothing but a series of insults, aggressions, and crimes; and Kṛṣṇa has determined, in his generous wisdom, to tolerate one hundred of them. In fact, there is no other aspect to their relationship: Śiśupāla—on his own behalf and undoubtedly on that of Jarāsandha whose armies he commands—persecutes Kṛṣṇa and his family, and Kṛṣṇa, the divine Kṛṣṇa, until the credit is exhausted, endures, withdraws, retreats, even abandons his capital before this madman. And, in the end, we see that underneath this evil-minded and perverse conduct, Śiśupāla hoped in the depth of his being only to be reunited with Kṛṣṇa-Viṣṇu, only to be one with him, like a Saint Paul who would have awaited death and the hereafter to find his road to Damascus.

More mystical than the epic, more willing to meditate on the sublime absurdities of theology, the Purāṇas have repeated, exploited, and clarified its matter. In the *Viṣṇu Purāṇa*, for example, the belief in metempsychosis allows the conflict to be prolonged:

from the standpoint of reincarnation, Śiśupāla is apparently a repeat offender with a checkered past. In previous lives, he has been the demon Hiraṇyakaśipu, and thereafter the demon Rāvaṇa, whom Viṣṇu killed in two of his incarnations. But it is in his new life as Śiśupāla that he has nursed against Kṛṣṇa, the incarnation of Viṣṇu, the most violent hatred. And precisely because of this violence, events this time around turn out differently, the routine of reincarnation has stopped, and another phenomenon occurs. In fact, all through his mature life Śiśupāla has only thought, spitefully to be sure, but in any case exclusively, of Viṣṇu; thanks to this obsession, in the end he is found ready, not for another random transmigration, but for the transformation which we have witnessed. The *Viṣṇu Purāṇa* explains[13] that, at the instant when he was killed by Viṣṇu, he was exposed for who he was, in his true nature; his furious hatred then evaporated, at the same time as the stock of sins he had accumulated, as if at will, was literally consumed by his venerable adversary. This made possible the happy, unexpected dénouement: total, definitive union of Śiśupāla and Kṛṣṇa-Viṣṇu, the reentry of the rebellious part into the immensely benevolent whole.

The reader has surely felt, granted all the differences imposed by divergence in time, place, civilization, and belief systems, how much this complex career, replete with strangeness, parallels that of Starkaðr. We should now give more precision to this impression.

[13] IV, 15, 1–5.

Viṣṇu as the man-lion (Narasiṃha) slays the demon Hiraṇyakaśipu, an earlier incarnation of Śiśupāla (relief from Ellora, India).

III

STARKAÐR AND ŚIŚUPĀLA

1. COMPARISON OF THE LEGENDS OF STARKAÐR AND ŚIŚUPĀLA

The stories of Starkaðr-Starcatherus and of Śiśupāla are readily arranged in parallel tables:

I	I
1. Starcatherus himself (in Saxo), or else the advance replica of Starkaðr, who is his homonymous grandfather (in the saga), is born outside the pale of human nature, a six- or eight-armed giant.	1. Śiśupāla is born outside of human nature, with four arms and three eyes, the latter trait (as well as his name) marking him as belonging to the god Rudra-Śiva.
2. With no explanation of how or even why, the god Thor relieves Starcatherus of his supernumerary arms and reduces him to human shape (Saxo); or Thor slays the grandfather Starkaðr, but the marks of the amputated arms linger on the otherwise	2. He is restored to human shape (two arms drop away, eye vanishes) at the touch of Kṛṣṇa-Viṣṇu, who, according to a Voice heard at his birth, will also be the agent of his death.

normal body of the grandson Starkaðr (saga).

II

1. Thereafter, it is another god, Othinus, and he alone, who concerns himself with him and determines his fate (Saxo); or else this fate is fixed, in an antagonistic debate, by the two gods Odin and Thor (saga);
2. In either case, the essential terms are that the hero will live three human lifetimes, but will commit a crime in each.

II

1. At that moment when he makes the small monster into a man, Kṛṣṇa-Viṣṇu declares his destiny:
2. since it is he, Kṛṣṇa, who is called upon to slay him, he consents to let pass unpunished one hundred offenses, each of which would merit death, thus acknowledging as inevitable that the humanized monster will commit offenses; at the hundred and first will come the end.

III

This triple life is, accordingly:

1. filled with martial exploits,
2. vitiated only by the three foreordained crimes,

III

Śiśupāla:

1. becomes the general of Jarāsandha, the conquering king whose armies subdue nearly the entire world; presumably he is, as general, the agent of at least several of these numerous victories;
2. at the same time, he adds up and pours on the offenses against Kṛṣṇa and his family, so that his credit of impunity is rapidly ex-

hausted; in the final indictment, Kṛṣṇa cites, as typical examples, five of these hundred offenses,

3. which are distributed among the three functions (first, then second, then third).

3. which are distributed among the three functions (two in the second function, one in the first, two in the third).

IV

1. The plot of Starcatherus develops particularly in his relations with King Frotho and his descendants, and its driving force is an uncompromising and aggressive reverence for royal majesty; imposing his exacting ideal of this majesty, he reprimands kings and their offspring;
2. and yet his three crimes, bad exceptions to a string of uniformly good deeds, are committed against kings, his kings.

IV

In the final scene of his life, where Śiśupāla is presented at length:

1. he makes himself the theorist and the determined, aggressive defender of royal majesty;
2. and yet, an allusion of Bhīṣma and the animated reaction of Śiśupāla himself lead one to believe that this attitude is destined only to plunge to their deaths the kings who are present; moreover, the five offenses enumerated by Kṛṣṇa injure, in various ways, a king.

V

Having committed the third and last of the foreordained crimes,

V

Having reached the number of one hundred offenses exempted from punishment because of the promise,

1. Starcatherus wishes to die, and to have himself beheaded chooses Hatherus, a young nobleman who has moreover revenge to take on him, and whose name and characteristics indicate that he is, in human form, the god Höðr, very close to Odin;	1. Śiśupāla, in a sort of madness, condemns himself by the hundred and first offense to die beheaded at the hand of Kṛṣṇa-Viṣṇu;
2. he heaps his good will upon this youth, and just before having himself killed by him, shows him the means (which the other, mistrusting, does not use) of gaining invulnerability by passing quickly between his trunk and severed head before they fall to the ground.	2. at the very moment when Kṛṣṇa-Viṣṇu has just decapitated him, his spiritual energy, attracted by his killer, enters into the latter in the form of light.

How are we to interpret this parallelism?

2. COMMON INHERITANCE?

In principle, accordances observed between the traditions of two human groups historically separate, but sprung from a single prehistoric group, can be explained in four ways: either by chance, or by innate and constant characteristics of the human spirit, or by direct or indirect borrowing, or by the preservation of a common inheritance. The first two explanations are here out of the question. The two tales which we have compared are too complex, and articulate in the same order too many peculiar and specific ideas, for such a structure plausibly to have been created twice. Furthermore, no inherent need in the human mind links themes as clearly independent as those which are brought together here: what innate connection is there between the fact that a monstrous giant, with too many arms, is restored to human form (or that the descendant of another giant has a human form, but is congenitally marked with such scars), and the fact that this giant or his descendant appoints himself champion of royal majesty? Or between this monstrosity, corrected or reduced to its hereditary marks, and a life either marked off or measured by a predetermined number of crimes? And one can pose the same question for practically all the episodes, taken two by two.

The explanation by borrowing is equally unlikely: the borrowing could only be indirect, and one does not see what intermediaries, peoples or individuals, could have effected it; neither the Scythians, nor the Slavs, nor the Turks had this lofty ideal of the "kingly function," and geographically, in the vast area which separates India and Scandinavia, no story has been found which could pass for a variant, even a very deformed one, of one or the other of these two so similar biographies. Further, we are dealing here not with a folktale pattern easily introduced into any civilization, but with an original narrative at once heroic and mythological, which gives rather the impression of being a work of learned literature —and such works do not travel easily. Finally and above all, what we observe in common between the two tales is the opposite of what is preserved, in fact it is exactly what is most easily lost, in a direct or indirect borrowing: save for the monstrous birth, no episode appears exactly the same in the two cases, with the same picturesque details; nothing in one of the two stories can be a mere copy of what it is in the other. Thus, the ways in which Starcatherus and Śiśupāla find themselves restored to human shape are completely different: in one case a violent operation, in the other a spontaneous process; and so with the agents of this miracle: Thor is the constant enemy of giants, Kṛṣṇa is the cousin of the small monster. The connection established, in both cases, between length of life and a certain number of crimes does not have the same form. The pairs of gods, openly or implicitly antagonistic, Thor and Odin, Rudra-Śiva and Kṛṣṇa-Viṣṇu, cannot be translations one of the other. The circumstances in which Starcatherus and Śiśupāla give their sermons on the majesty of kings have nothing in common: the one prevents his king from hazarding himself against an enemy who is no king, then becomes tutor of the royal children; the other protests against an honor paid before kings to one who is not a king. To be sure the violent, wounding rhetoric of the two characters finds at times rather similar expressions, but their orientations are different: Starcatherus inveighs against Ingellus in order to reform him, Śiśupāla reviles Kṛṣṇa to humiliate him. Even in the list of sins according to the three functions, the correspondences of each sin to its function are not congruent: at the third level, Śiśupāla's lust is sexual, that of Starcatherus is, so to speak, monetary; at the second level, Starcatherus flees on the battlefield, Śiśupāla profits basely from the absence of a king by sacking his town; and at the first level, Śiśupāla hinders a king from sacrificing, Starkaðr-Starcatherus furnishes the king, his master, as the victim in a human sacrifice. The impulses which drive the two heroes—one triply old, the other in full strength—to their executioners do not have the same source: Śiśupāla acts in a sort of madness; Starcatherus has decided, calmly, to put an end to what a Mallarméan might well describe as "trop de vie"; if it is indeed the god Höðr who lurks in the person of Hatherus, Starcatherus' killer, he has nothing in common, at first sight, with Viṣṇu, and the decapitation scene, calm and serene in Saxo, is a climax of violence in the *Mahābhārata*. Finally, the last scenes have undoubtedly similar values, but only similar: to interpret matters in the best light, Starcatherus, in a gesture of benevolence, wishes to transfer to the friend who beheads him something of himself which will assure him invulnerability; Śiśupāla, suddenly captivated by the enemy who beheads him, wishes to merge, and in fact does dissolve into him in the form of a flame escaping from his body.

Thus, in every episode, the circumstances, and often the relationships of the characters, differ from one story to the other. The agreement, palpable and striking, is elsewhere: in the common ideas which underpin entirely parallel plots couched in generally different narratives. Such a situation would suffice to discourage the hypothesis of a loan, even if it were geographically conceivable. There remains that of two evolutions starting from a common original. As a first approximation, we can establish this framework as follows:

I

1–2. A being, who will be a hero, is born outside of human form, with monstrosities, superfluous organs, which relate him to the most disquieting element in mythology; but this deformity is corrected, and the infant is restored to human shape either by the act or by the touch of the god who is normally the adversary of demonical beings. Variant: a being, who will be a hero, is born as the posthumous and homonymous grandson of such a monster who has been not "pruned" but slain by the god inimical to demons (giants), and bears the hereditary marks of the limbs cut from his grandfather.

II

1. Two gods explicitly (Thor and Odin, Kṛṣṇa-Viṣṇu, all in human form) or implicitly (Rudra-Śiva), from without (through decisions) or within (through his own nature), vie for the hero or confront each other over him: the one harboring a weakness for the sort of monster which, although corrected, the hero continues to carry within him, and the other whose calling is to subdue or destroy such monsters.

2. The upshot for the hero is the announcement of a fate linking his longevity to the completion of a specific number of crimes, either that he will be allowed to go on living as long as he does not exceed this number, or that he is granted a prolonged but limited (thrice normal) life span, while being compelled to commit one crime in each segment.

III

The life thus ordained—flexible or multiple—is (1) full of exploits, (2) highlighted by the predestined crimes, and (3) these crimes (or the most characteristic among them) occur successively at each of the three functional levels.

IV

The warrior on whom this ambiguous destiny weighs (1) professes to honor and defend the rights and the majesty of kings, and (2) nevertheless offends a king by each of his crimes.

V

The predestined number of crimes having been committed, (1) the warrior brings on his own death, and by request or by committing an additional offense, has himself beheaded by a god who is either identical with the one who determined the length of his life or is theologically very close to him. (2) At the moment of decapitation, he transfers (or desires to transfer) to his killer an essential part of his inner being.

3. RUDRA AND VIṢṆU

Thrown back thus upon the hypothesis of a common inheritance, the interpretation meets with a certain number of problems, some proposed by the divergences, others by the very parallels themselves. The overriding problem concerns the Scandinavian and Indian divinities, more precisely the pairs of divinities who intervene in the hero's life, Odin and Thor, Rudra-Śiva and Kṛṣṇa-Viṣṇu. These dyads are, at first glance, far removed from each other: are not the magical sovereign Odin and Thor the champion above all, in contrast to the opulent and sensual Vanir, the first and second entries on the canonical list of the gods of the three functions?[1] Rudra and Viṣṇu, in contrast, well attested in the ṚgVeda, neither associate with nor confront each other, and do not form any structure;[2] it is only Hinduism that will develop their opposi-

[1] *Gods of the Ancient Northmen* (1973), chap. 1; *ME I*, p. 288 and n. 1.

[2] Another component of Śiva, Śarva (important hymns in the *Atharva-Veda*), is Indo-Iranian. That still other components may have come from the civilization of

tion as destroyer and savior in the periodical world crises; in any case, at no time are they defined by any connection with two different levels of the trifunctional structure: the Vedic Viṣṇu is above all an associate of Indra at the second level, and the polymorphous activity of Rudra does not allow of expression within the framework of this structure; as healer, as herbalist, he operates on the third level, and as archer, alone or in his plural form *Rudrāḥ*, also on the second, while nothing seems to orient him toward the sovereign level. How is one to understand that pairs of such divergent makeup can be injected with equal ease and co-exist comfortably within the same plot?

Even if we were forced to dwell upon this view, the difficulty would not be as great as it seems: one would in fact conceive the plot as having implied only that the hero was somehow spread-eagled between two opposing rival divinities, the motive for this opposition mattering little and being liable to change, with no harm done, in the course of time. Originally, for example, the two divinities might have been what they still are in Scandinavia, those of the two highest functional levels (magical sovereign and warrior), while in post-Vedic India, where the living theology no longer thought in terms of the trifunctional framework, they were replaced by the pair whose conflict was at that time the most obvious and interesting for men, that of Śiva and Viṣṇu. Sure enough. But internal criticism would easily raise objections: it is clear that Thor and Odin—supposedly old in the Scandinavian narrative—do not contend for Starkaðr merely as "champion" and "magical sovereign." According to the saga, each of the two gods grants gifts and determines fates, and Odin's magic hardly has occasion to appear, save in the metamorphoses of the cord and the wand which strangle and pierce Vikar on the occasion of the first felony. Among Odin's

---

Mohenjo-Daro is possible, although in this case more sanguine assertions than proofs are presented; see most recently Asko Parpola, Seppo Koskenniemi, Simo Parpola, and Pentti Aalto, *Decipherment of the Proto-Dravidian Inscriptions of the Indus Civilization* (1969), pp. 5–6 and nn. 10–21; *Progress in the Decipherment of the Proto-Dravidian Indus Script* (1969), pp. 9–11, 15–18 (and 18–20, Kṛṣṇa!) and nn. 9–22, 23–50. Cf. below, p. 84, n. 7.

gifts, only poetry could be strictly connnected with his magical function; all the rest, prolonged life, victory in every battle, the favor of the great, personal wealth, etc., are located elsewhere. Finally, from Ódin as sovereign one would expect some promotion of his protégé on the scale of power; on the contrary Starkaðr remains constantly and systematically at the second rank, and though he holds to the creed of royal majesty, he does not himself pretend to it. He reforms, avenges, and exceptionally, in his three *facinora,* slays kings, but he never seeks to replace them.

As for the Indian legend, nothing allows one to think that, at an earlier stage, the two gods who oppose each other concerning Śiśupāla had been the canonical patrons of the first two functions, the Vedic and the pre-Vedic Varuṇa and Indra. If Varuṇa's development has greatly reduced his importance and deprived him of his functional rank, Indra on the contrary has remained alive and has even extended his power in epic mythology—where he is the king of the gods—and has not been shorn of his own adventures: why, in this particular case, should he have given way to Viṣṇu?

Having discarded this simplistic solution, we must return to the texts themselves, to observation of the *modus operandi* which they attribute to the two gods.

First, let us consider the Indian tale from the point of view of the ordinary mythology of the epic where it is found. Rudra-Śiva, we have said, works implicity, from within Śiśupāla. The child is born monstrous, in the god's image, and he bears a name that is like the diminutive of *paśupati,* a distinctive epithet of the god. By this affinity, almost possession, he is bound to oppose Kṛṣṇa-Viṣṇu and to die at his hand, as the Voice heard at his birth, and the miracle worked upon Kṛṣṇa's knees, interpreted consistently, declare for him. This is known well by Kṛṣṇa, who with the baby still on his lap foresees that he will have to receive and tolerate from him a total of a hundred offenses. Besides these Rudraic traits, Śiśupāla carries moreover the heredity, or at least the ancestry of a demon, since he is—already in the Mahābhārata—the reincarnation of the character who appears successively as Hiraṇyakaśipu and Rāvaṇa, two terrible demons whose destruction necessitated prior incarnations of Viṣṇu, and the first of whom, it has been said, "represents Śivaism."[3]

This dual nature, which makes him a little Śiva and at the same time a demonic being, governs everything else, and particularly the actions of the gods in the story. Śiva, who is himself not demoniacal, but assumes, in the life of the universe, the disagreeable but necessary function of destroyer, liquidator, thus the "primus motor" of regeneration, nonetheless has a marked predilection for great demons. Opposing him, Viṣṇu always bides his time, and when it comes, puts an end to the outrage of a victorious demon whom his colleague has put up with, sometimes at the price of being the first to suffer from it. Here one may read with profit the end of the excellent description composed nearly two centuries ago by a virtually forgotten observer, the Colonel de Polier, of the relations between Śiva and the demons, or as he calls them, *Mhadaio* [Mahādeva, Śiva] and the *Daints* [*daityas*, demons].[4]

> "Most of the time, according to the tales, the disciples of this *Deiotas* [*devatā*, divinity] named *Gan* [*gaṇas*, troops of spirits] are the *Daints*.
>
> Raven, tyrant of Lanca, whose crimes and oppression occasioned the seventh incarnation of Viṣṇu, was a zealous admirer of Mhadaio. He offered him his head in sacrifice. The Deiotas repaid him with ten more of them, and this Daints having again sacrificed them to his celestial patron, the latter, moved by gratitude for such constant devotion, thought he

[3] Edward. W. Hopkins, op. cit., p. 211.

[4] *Mythologie des Indous, travaillée par Mme la Chnesse de Polier, sur des manuscrits authentiques apportés de l'Inde par feu M. le Colonel de Polier, Membre de la Société asiatique de Calcutta*, Roudolstadt and Paris, 2 vols. (1809) (see below, Appendix). The colonel had collected the material around 1780 from his informant the Pundit Rāmacandra ("Ramtchund"); his cousin presented it in the form of Ramtchund's explanations, set off by judicious questions or remarks from his pupil; see *ME I*, pp. 42–44. The passage quoted here is in I, 221–223.

could only acquit himself towards his devotee by endowing him with the property such that to whatever degree a limb should be cut from him, it would reappear instantly, and that he could not be put to death save until nine hundred million nine hundred thousand heads should be cut from him, the which rendered the defeat of this monster so difficult that it was necessary for Viṣṇu himself to be incarnated to purge the earth of him."

"I had thought until now," said Monsieur de Polier, "that the multitude of heads and arms with which your great *deiotas* are represented was their exclusive attribute."

"No," answered the Teacher, "this is not at all one of the marks of their superiority, for the Daints in the first three epochs are almost all endowed with heads and arms infinitely, and nearly all with invulnerability; and although these prerogatives are most of the time the gifts of Mhadaio, nevertheless their extraordinary strength, the attribute of their gigantic race, gives them already so much pride, ambition, and means of doing evil that there is no one but Viṣṇu who could correct or destroy them.

The Rajah Bhanasser, in his devotions addressed to Mhadaio, had so often repeated the offering of his head, and the recompense accorded by the Deiotas had also been so often renewed, that the wearied Mhadaio at last entreated his servant to moderate his zeal, by which he had acquired such an excess of strength and pride that after having subjugated the earth and the heavens, he complained that there no longer existed any being against whom he could try his strength. Touched by his misery, Mhadaio consoled him by predicting that Viṣṇu in one of his incarnations would do him the honor of fighting with him. Indeed the battle took place, and the Daints, losing one after another of his heads and arms, also lost his pride and became a sincere devotee of Viṣṇu."

"From these tales it seems," said M. de Polier, "that Mhadaio is the protector and avowed friend of the Daints."

"At least," replied the Pundit, "in none of the generally admitted tales does one see him incarnated as Viṣṇu for the purpose of destroying this evil race. And although his votaries claim that he has appeared to his devotees in a thousand and eight different forms, nonetheless one finds in the tales which comprise the account of the Purāṇas no detailed history of these appearances, nor the character which the mythology attributes to a true incarnation and which is, as I have told you, the birth of the Deiotas in a human or animal body to fulfil a general aim important to the well-being of mankind and directly influence the events and actions which restore order and virtue on the earth. In judging in this regard the appearances of Mhadaio, one sees that they are only transitory, restricted to his devotees, and that they appear rather transformations or metamorphoses of a magician than incarnations of a divinity."

This presentation, consistent with the epic and Purāṇic mythology, expresses the essence and sufficiently explains the roles and relationships of the hero and the two gods. But that cannot be enough for us. We must go back further, albeit hypothetically, since the comparison with the saga of Starcatherus proves that the material of the story of Śiśupāla considerably antedates the version which we read in the epic.

Let us note first that it is not so certain, at least in settings other than those where the Vedic hymns and prose treatises were composed, that the opposition of Rudra and Viṣṇu was not already present as a structure. In an earlier work, we have seen in outline, beneath the heroic transposition presented by the *Mahābhārata*, a mythology which is very old and more complete than the Vedic one, entailing for example an eschatology: the destruction, then salvaging of the Kuru dynasty have been overlaid on a myth of cosmic crisis—the end of one world and the beginning of another—whose pre-Vedic character is guaranteed by Iranian and especially Scandinavian parallels; its agents are Aśvatthāman for the destruction and Kṛṣṇa for the salvation, that is clearly Rudra-Śiva and Viṣṇu incarnate.[5] In the Vedic hymns themselves, although Rudra (one of the most important future components of Śiva) is not set dramatically in opposition, or theologically in diptych with

[5] *ME I*, pp. 208–245.

Viṣṇu, the functions of the two gods are nevertheless contradictory, and in a way which prefigures the epic version. The main service which Viṣṇu renders to Indra, whose assistant he is, and also to other gods and even to mankind sprung from Manu, is, by steps beginning with the famous "three steps" which he takes in so many mythological and ritual contexts, to give them their working or living space, as if this acreage (root *mā-*) would add to their domain, to the domain of Order, portions of space which at first eluded them.[6] In this role, he is quite the opposite of the Vedic Rudra, whose traits were disentangled by the careful study of Ernst Arbman:[7] Rudra is the patron of all that has not yet been domesticated by man or society, hence the master all at once of the hazards and risks inherent in the wilderness of the vast unexplored country which surrounds the little haunts of men, their narrow roads and vulnerable crossroads; the master of the bush, with its aberrant population of ascetics as well as brigands, an extension of the chaos at the fringe and sometimes even at the heart of civilized lands, with its monsters, its myriad plants, the powers of poison and cure it holds in store; the master, more generally, of what at any time and under any circumstances of life is analogous to the wild, of all that men want to make their own but have not yet brought to pass, and which holds the mystery and ambiguity of the un-begun: the new dish or linen, the meal that is only barely prepared, the enterprise that is only planned. Such seems to have been the original nature of this Rudra whose name is best explained by the root of the Latin *rudis* "rough, unpolished," and who is easily split up into an infinity of *Rudrās* each attached to such a road, object, etc. Concealed in the forest or on the mountain, he is at the same time the persecutor whose lethal arrow arrives from some unknown direction, and the knower of remedies, of herbs which destroy illness. Not evil, but morally neutral, at once powerful and undetermined.

[6] "Víṣṇu et les Marút à travers la réforme zoroastrienne," *Journal asiatique* CCXLII (1953), 1–25.

[7] *Rudra, Untersuchungen zum altindischen Glauben und Kultus* (1922); cf. *Archaic Roman Religion* (1970), pp. 418–419.

If these characteristics of Viṣṇu and Rudra are valid for the Vedic texts, it is probable that in more ancient times, during and before the migrations which led bands of Indo-Europeans to the Five Rivers, the two divinities conceived in this way were even more important: Ind(a)ra gave victory to the conquerors, but it was Viṣṇu who opened the way for him, and through him, opened the way for them through the unknown, barbarous realm where, besides demons, there already lived a god of their tribe, the alarming and necessary Rudra. Well before the composition of the *Sabhāparvan*, before the amplification and elevation of Rudra-Śiva and Viṣṇu by the classical mythology, at a time when the epic material may well have been a "fifth Veda," the story of Śiśupāla could therefore have existed essentially as we read it, presenting the same gods. Born with those superfluous arms and eye, Śiśupāla is the product of an exuberance, an excess of nature; he reproduces the figure of Rudra-Śiva, and above all, Rudra-Śiva can take pleasure in him: he is of his domain. Viṣṇu tames him by his mere touch, that is, he adapts him, at least in physical appearance, to life in society, making of him a normal human being. But within, he is not transformed for all that, and the conflict goes on between this incorrigible outsider and the saving, restoring, regulating god, until the moment when it is Viṣṇu, the civilized one, who prevails, and emerging from his long forbearance, puts an end to the challenger's perpetual aggression. But, at this very instant, the challenger is enlightened, the outsider is converted and becomes a part of Viṣṇu, as all land wrested from the bush becomes a portion of the village or the kingdom.

4. ODIN AND THOR

Let us imagine the reverse, an ideology where the disquieting Rudra would dominate this confrontation and would have the last word in it, where Rudra would be more prestigious if not more powerful than Viṣṇu—and we shall be very close to the explanation of the career of Starcatherus.

Spending many years exploring all over the Indo-European world mythological derivatives, as well as deformations, of the trifunctional structure, I have too exclusively defined Odin as a Scandinavian Varuṇa. So he is, to be sure, and in the *Hárbarðsljóð* for example, his opposition to Thor, with the often offensive stichomachy which expresses it, is well illuminated by the Vedic texts where Varuṇa and Indra boastingly confront each other, the magical and terrible sovereign on one side, the prestigious champion on the other. But the rich nature of Odin is not exhausted by this formula.[8]

Within the trifunctional structure itself, I myself have many times pointed out the evolution, peculiar to the Germanic world, by which war has, so to speak, overflowed from the warrior level to the sovereign level: much more than Thor, Odin concerns himself with battle and combatants, with the fighting aristocracy at the very least; Thor is rather the solitary, irresistible champion, a sort of Vāyu or Bhīma whose chief exploit, moreover—storm, thunder and rain—attracts to him the worship of the peasant, while Odin is interested in the people in arms (which was the normal state of many a Germanic society) and in the commander of the army. There is a kind of slippage in the terms of the canonical list of the Scandinavian gods, compared with those of the Vedic hymns and rituals:[9]

(1)	Varuṇa }	Odin	(1) and (2)
(2)	{ Indra } / Vāyu }		
(3)	fertility gods }	{ Thor	(2) and (3)
		{ fertility gods	(3)

[8] *Gods of the Ancient Northmen* (1973), chap. 2.

[9] Cf. "The Rigsþula and Indo-European Social Structure" in *Gods of the Ancient Northmen*, pp. 118–125.

But this is not yet all. Following Jakob Wilhelm Hauer (1927), Rudolf Otto (1932) and Jan de Vries (1957) have listed an impressive number of traits, physical and mental, of character and behavior, by which Odin is rather homologous with Rudra.[10] Not all are convincing, some are not even exact, but important ones remain: both are tireless wanderers, they like to appear to men only in disguise, unrecognizable, Odin with a hat pulled down to his eyes, Rudra with his *uṣnīṣa* falling over his face; Odin is the master of the runes as Rudra is *kavi*; and above all the bands of Rudra's devotees, bound by a vow, endowed with powers and privileges, recall sometimes the *berserkir*, sometimes the *einherjar* of Odin. This sovereign god, this magician, unarguably has one of his bases in the mysterious region where the savage borders on the civilized. Like Rudra-Śiva, he is often, in terms of ordinary rules, even immoral—and Thor is not shy about so telling him when they trade charges. Like Rudra-Śiva, he has his taste for human sacrifice, particularly the self-sacrifice of his votaries.[11] More generally, like Rudra-Śiva, he has in him something almost demonic: his friendship and weakness for Loki are well known; but Loki is the malicious rogue who, one fine day, in arranging the murder of Baldr, takes on the dimensions of a "spirit of evil," of the greatest evil.[12]

Among the North Germanics, demons primarily appear as the giants. With them too, Odin has more than one connection. On his father's side he is descended, through very few intermediate generations, from a rather singular giant, as a matter of fact the primordial giant, Ymir, and his mother is the very daughter of a giant with the disquieting name Bölþorn, 'Spine of woe.' Many times he evinces a strangely conciliatory, pacifist feeling regarding the worst giants, and it then requires the intervention of Thor to extricate

[10] Jakob Wilhelm Hauer, *Der Vrātya, Untersuchungen über nichtbrahmanische Religion Altindiens,* I (1927), 189–240 ("Die Vrātya als śivaitische Bacchanten"); Rudolf Otto, *Gottheit und Gottheiten der Arier* (1932), pp. 58–60; Jan de Vries, *Altgermanische Religionsgeschichte*² (1957), pp. 95–96.

[11] Cf. "Hanging and Drowning," appendix I to *From Myth to Fiction* (1973).

[12] See Dumézil, *Loki* (Paris, 1948); German edition, 1959.

him, by killing the giant, from the predicament in which this disposition has placed him, along with the other gods: thus he has led Hrungnir within the walls of the Æsir, and the giant threatens to walk off with everything, provisions and the most beautiful goddesses, and he would do it did not Thor, invoked *in extremis* by the gods, intervene.[13] All this is truly Śivaistic. Let us read again Polier's description:[14]

> A famous Daints, named Basmagut [= ?], was curious to know which of the three Deiotas [Brahma, Viṣṇu, Śiva] surpassed him in greatness and strength. He consulted Nardman [Nāradamuni], who replied that it was Mhadaio [Mahādeva = Rudra-Śiva]. . . .
>
> Basmagut, wishing to profit from the instructions of Nardman, began his sacrifice [to Mhadaio, by mutilating himself]. The Deiotas, flattered by the zeal and earnestness which the Daints showed in his service, appeared to him accompanied by Parbutty [Parvatī]. At the mere sight of Mhadaio, not only was the mutilated body of the Daints returned to its natural state, but he received also from the Deiotas the power of reducing to ashes any objects on which he placed his hands with the intention of consuming them. Meanwhile the sight and the charms of Parbutty inspired in the Daints the most violent passion, and this being, as ungrateful as he was wicked, saw no other means of ridding himself of an inconvenient spouse than to use against Mhadaio himself the gift which he had received from him. The Deiotas, who perceives the intentions of Basmagut, evades him, but the Daints pursues him. By now Mhadaio, nearly being caught, knows no more how to escape him, and in the anguish which he feels sees no other recourse than to repair to Viṣṇu who, immediately assuming the shape of Parbutty, appears before the Daints; and, pretending to be susceptible to his advances, assures him that she prefers him to her lout of a husband, who is forever

[13] *Skáldskaparmál,* 25 (= *Edda Snorra Sturlusonar,* ed. Finnur Jónsson [1931], pp. 100–103); cf. *The Destiny of the Warrior* (1970), pp. 157–160.

[14] I, 221–223 (see above, p. 81, n. 4)

drunk, surrounded by snakes, and apt to inspire disgust rather than love. "Nevertheless," adds the false Parbutty, "he has in his way of dancing such an irresistible charm that then all his ugliness vanishes to my eyes." At these words Basmagut, transported with joy over the favorable inclination that Parbutty showed him, wants to win further favor in her eyes and insists that she teach him the dance she is speaking of. She agrees and the lesson begins. But Viṣṇu, in the guise of the Deiotany [goddess], takes care to thicken the Maya [the *māyā*] or cloud thrown over the Daints' senses, so that he completely forgets the deadly gift he received from Mhadaio, and has no thought but to follow and imitate the movements of the fake Parbutty. He sees her carelessly put a hand on her head, does the same, and instantly reduces himself to ashes.

However satisfied Viṣṇu was to have delivered his colleague from the danger to which the latter had exposed himself, he reproached him for his imprudence. "I agree," answered Mhadaio, "I cannot resist the devotions of my worshippers, although I know full well that most of the time they make very ill use of my favors. But," he added, "I place my trust in you, your indulgence supports my weakness, it does not permit me to suffer from my own improvidence." After doing this homage to Viṣṇu, he intoned a hymn in praise of him.

As opposed to Odin, Thor, all of a piece, is rigor itself. His relationships with the giants are summed up in one word: he exterminates them by his extreme strength, aided only occasionally by the ruse of a companion, Loki or Thjalfi. His constant mission is to save the gods and the world by destroying this brood. A Viṣṇu minus the charm, he performs it without subtlety or compromise.

We see how, though it does not match the relationship of Rudra-Śiva and Viṣṇu, that of Odin and Thor covers to an extent the same ground. The overriding difference is that Viṣṇu—in the only sense that matters here—is superior to Rudra-Śiva, even constituting his ultimate recourse, while Odin, notwithstanding his imprudences with the giants, is superior to Thor, hierarchically speaking and apparently also in the degree of esteem accorded him by human society. His complexity, his magical knowledge, the posthumous happiness he assures his followers in Valhöll, all make him theologically more interesting. Thor is invoked in present dangers, honored on high-seat pillars as the watchful guardian of dwellings, given thanks for the rain that fertilizes the fields, but he does not have at his disposal the large assortment of favors, especially the more mysterious ones, which enable Odin, with all his shortcomings, to remain until Ragnarök the highest god, the true sovereign. These observations allow us to understand the role of the divine pair in the story of Starkaðr. By the mere fact that Starkaðr is a giant or the grandson of a giant, he has Thor against him. Moreover, it is natural that the god who everywhere reestablishes the threatened order does not tolerate his monstrosity. Odin on the other hand takes offense neither at membership in the race of giants nor at the traces left behind by extra arms: just as he rides an eight-legged steed born of a giant's horse,[15] in the same way he can make use of this disturbing superman, and to this end takes him to a certain extent under his protection; he relies on him for a questionable deed, a human sacrifice whose victim, a king, is not consenting, and he rewards this crime with the gift of three lives.

Our observations also allow us to specify at what points, regarding the role of the gods, and consequently that of the hero, the stories of Starkaðr and Śiśupāla agree, and where they diverge. If for convenience we call Odin and Rudra-Śiva the "dark gods," and Thor and Viṣṇu the "light gods," each of the two heroes, by nature, belongs entirely to the dark god and is opposed by the light god. But the structures are almost reversed by the fact that in Scandinavia the dark god holds the first place, being more important in this

[15] *Gylfaginning*, 26 (= *Edda Snorra*, ed. F. Jónsson, pp. 45–47); see Jan de Vries, *Altgermanische Religionsgeschichte*², II (1957), 63–64, and Mircea Eliade, *Le Chamanisme*² (1969), pp. 300, 302, 304 n. 3 (on the horse Sleipnir), 364–365 (on eight-legged horses in Siberia, Japan, etc.). Besides Starkaðr, Sleipnir is the only example in the Scandinavian myths of a being endowed with an abnormal number of limbs.

life and especially in that to come, and that consequently his favor is the more desirable, the light god having only an immediate and limited range; whereas in the Indian legend it is the light god who is in the spotlight and directs the game, and whose favor in this life and in the hereafter is most fervently sought, while the dark god acts only implicitly, without showing himself, through the "Rudraic" nature of the hero. The result is that Starkaðr is, on the whole, a good hero, Śiśupāla an evil one. Obedient to the theology, the reader gives his sympathy to Starkaðr, and withholds it from Śiśupāla. This orientation continues in the conclusion of the two tales. The god into whom, at the instant of his decapitation, the hero transfuses (or wishes to transfuse) the most valuable part of himself is in India the light god, in Scandinavia, if not the dark god himself (Odin), then at least—downgraded to a young man—a god of his circle, and one of the closest (Höðr); the highest happiness consists, on one side, in merging with Viṣṇu, on the other in rejoining the world of Odin.

5. THE ROLES OF THE GODS IN THE TWO LEGENDS

Two superimposed tables will usefully summarize the foregoing considerations by assigning to each of the homologous gods his corresponding part in the character and behavior of the hero.

After the gigantic and monstrous (with supernumerary arms) birth (Saxo) or descent (saga) of the hero,

	Odin:	*Höðr:	Thor:
I.	—	—	Thor restores the hero to human

	Odin:	*Höðr:	Thor:
			form either directly, by amputation (Saxo), or indirectly, via the killing of his homonymous grandfather (saga).
II.	Odin grants the hero his three lives and imposes on him the three crimes, with other, good lots (Saxo); or: Odin grants the hero three lives with other, good lots (saga),	———	and Thor imposes on the hero the three crimes, along with other evil lots (saga).
III.	Through one of his gifts, Odin is responsible for the hero's many victories (Saxo & saga),	———	and, through one of his lots, Thor is responsible for the hero's terrible wounds (saga).
	Odin is responsible for the three crimes (distributed across the three		

	Odin:	*Höðr:	Thor:
	functions) and particularly the first, which he orders, directs and completes (Saxo);		
	or:—	—	Thor is responsible for the three crimes.
	the first of them (the only one recounted in the saga) is ordered, directed and completed by Odin (saga).		
IV.	As god of kings, Odin is undoubtedly responsible for the hero's royalist ideology, violated only in the three crimes (in Saxo and partly the saga).		
V.	—	The third crime done, the hero urges Hatherus to behead him, and wishes to transmit to Hatherus a power of his being by having him pass between his head and torso (Saxo)	

	[Rudra-Śiva, implicitly]:	Kṛṣṇa
I.	R., in his preceding incarnations, has protected the demon of whom the hero is the last incarnation. The hero is born in the monstrous shape of R. (extra arms and eye) and receives the name *Śiśupāla*, a calque on R.'s epithet *Paśu-pati*; ——	Kṛṣṇa, by his touch, restores the baby to human shape.
II.	The hero's "Rudraic" tendency destines him to offend Kṛṣṇa, ——	and Kṛṣṇa grants the hero impunity which will guarantee his life up to the hundredth offense.
III.	Through the protection he accords to the king whose general the hero is, R. is responsible for the hero's multiple victories, many of which are won at the expense of Kṛṣṇa. Through the hero's "Rudraic" orientation, R. is responsible for the quick accomplishment of the hundred offenses against Kṛṣṇa, particularly the five characteristic ones (distributed over the three functions).	

	[Rudra-Śiva, implicitly]:	Kṛṣṇa
IV.	[see the following chapter]	
V.	———	The hundred offenses accomplished, the hero by a hundred and first offense provokes Kṛṣṇa into beheading him, and, emerging from his decapitated body, the hero's spiritual energy flows into Kṛṣṇa in the form of light.

The reader will note that one section of this table, the fourth, remains obscure. It will be made clear in the next chapter, by further considerations, but however it may be explained, and setting aside the role of the gods, the fact itself is certain: Śiśupāla and Starkaðr appear as the defenders of the rights and the majesty of kings, and yet turn their crimes against these rights and this majesty. If, as we have been led to admit, these two figures and their histories go back to a time when the ancestors of the Germanics and those of the Indic peoples were neighbors somewhere between the Baltic and the Black Sea, this fact is important. It reveals a feature of the royal ideology of the most ancient Indo-Europeans, or at least a part of them: the champion's ambiguous attitude toward the king, or as Tacitus would have said, of the *dux* towards the *rex*, had already produced epic tales.

To be sure, in the versions we read, kingship is adjusted according to place and time. The Frotho whom Starcatherus protects, whose children he reforms, the Wicarus and Olo Vegetus whom he betrays and kills, are modelled either on the Danish kings of the twelfth and thirteenth centuries,[16] or on the Viking kings who

[16] *From Myth to Fiction* (1973), introduction to Appendix 2 ("Gram").

had prospered during the preceding centuries; and these forms of kingship, especially the first, are more majestic, more firmly established, than those described in the *Germania*. The royalty whose prestige Śiśupāla defends is epic kingship, which we do not see taking shape under our eyes like that of Valdemar (India has no history), but which is certainly quite different, but also more solemn and imperial, than what we can glimpse of Vedic kingships. But these changes are expected; to survive the course of time, a mythical or legendary record of kingship is inevitably and constantly colored by prevailing tastes, from one century and one period to another. All that the comparison of the two stories compels us to admit is that, from Indo-European times, with a more archaic and undoubtedly fragile, as well as more magical status, kingship was considered the highest value, in no way comparable with other levels of society, which latter may have been more powerful and even threatening in practice, but were ideologically inferior. What is so surprising in this? Did not every Vedic and Scandinavian petty king, whatever his weakness, have as his patron god the all-powerful master of the universe, Varuṇa or Odin?

As for the fact itself that a complex and subtle royal ideology, laden with legends, had existed among the Indo-Europeans before their dispersal and had survived in the "daughter" societies, this has been established by previous studies;[17] the present one merely supports it with a new example. I shall be content with directing the reader to another study,[18] to the astonishing correspondence of the Indian Yayāti, with his sons, his daughter Mādhavī and his ephemeral sons-in-law, and the Irish Eochaid Feidlech, with his sons, his daughter Medb and his unstable sons-in-law. If the Germans have lost or not known the word **rēg-* and given the king a different name, they have nonetheless preserved, as we see here, complex legends which illustrate aspects of the kingly function.

[17] To mention only accordances between the Vedic *rājan* and the Roman *rēg-*, see *Archaic Roman Religion* (1970), pp. 224–228 (the *aśvamedha* and the October Horse), pp. 583–585 (the *rex*, the *Brahmán*, and the *flamines maiores).*

[18] *The Destiny of a King* (1973).

IV

JARĀSANDHA

1. ODIN, RUDRA-ŚIVA AND THE SACRIFICED KINGS

It is obvious that the relationships between the hero and the kings are the most coherent in the Scandinavian story.

Starcatherus is not a king himself, he serves kings. His lofty ideal of the kingly function is that of a high-level servant, equally capable, according to circumstances, of serving as his master's bodyguard or as tutor of his children. Even in the three crimes which he is bound to commit he never evinces the slightest wish to usurp: in the murder of Vikar he merely helps Odin, and if he kills Olo Vegetus, his failing is one of venality, not of ambition. Śiśupāla, on the contrary, is a king, a king among those gathered around the son of Pāṇḍu for the *rājasūya*. From the scene he makes when Kṛṣṇa, who is no king, finds himself singled out for special honors, one has the impression that he feels in the first place personally offended, and that he generalizes his grievance, speaking in the name of all the assembled kings, merely as a device rather generally used in such situations.

Likewise, if the five exemplary crimes which Kṛṣṇa singles out are aimed against kings, none is the chief crime of regicide. His "first-function crime" does affect the king in the domain of the sacred, on the occasion of a sacrifice which would have increased the king's prestige and which he makes impossible by stealing the victim, but this victim is only a horse. Starcatherus, in contrast, in two of his crimes, kills a king who is his master, and the first of the crimes consists in "sending" Odin, at his insistence, King Vikar, that is, sacrificing the latter by means of a deception in which Starcatherus is the god's accomplice.

Thus we are led to think that the Scandinavian version, on these two points, is more conservative—the more so since human sacrifice, attested in Scandinavia until the conversion to Christianity, is certainly something archaic, and hence, when it is found in a story, there is little chance of its having been added after the fact. But we have proof that India, on these same two points, has in fact modified the plot, and we can understand the cause of these changes: the history of Śiśupāla must not be considered alone, it forms the second panel of a diptych of which the first is no less interesting. Śiśupāla's verbal attack, at the very moment when Yudhiṣṭhira is at last about to celebrate his *rājasūya*, is in fact only the second and last obstacle confronting the ceremony. There has been another one, just before the beginning of the preparations.

When Yudhiṣṭhira deems that the moment has come to celebrate this sacrifice, understood here, we recall, as an imperial act conferring on the sacrificer primacy over all kings, he consults Kṛṣṇa, who approves it, but warns him of a problem. There is another king, namely Jarāsandha of Magadha, who has already realized in practice, without sacrifice, the object of the *rājasūya*, and has subjugated most of the kings.[1] And how has he gained this success? Certainly his general has had no small part in it (574):[2]

> "Another king, the mighty Śiśupāla, has gone over completely to his side and has indeed, wise prince, become his marshal."

Thus, though a king, Śiśupāla finds here, in the service of another king, the rank and function which Starcatherus holds under several kings.

[1] *Mahābhārata*, pp. 57–66 (śl. 559–767).

[2] Reminding one of the words of Marshal Joffre, when some people disputed his credentials as the victor of the Marne: "They don't know who won the battle? I know well enough who would have lost it!"

Kṛṣṇa then resumes the history of these campaigns, several of which have been directed against the Yādavas—Kṛṣṇa's family—and one of which has even forced them to leave the country, and he names the great warriors whom Jarāsandha has had at his command; to this point we have only the description of a conqueror, like so many others, whom Yudhiṣṭhira must eliminate if he wishes to be able to celebrate his imperial sacrifice. But Jarāsandha is unique. His victories, ensured by his general, have a solemn foundation and a cruel outcome (627–629):

> "After he had defeated them all, he imprisoned the kings in his mountain corral, Girivraja, as a lion imprisons great elephants in a cave of the Himālaya. King Jarāsandha wants to sacrifice the lords of the earth. . . ."

Sacrifice to what god? To Rudra-Śiva, to Mahādeva, to whom he owes his victories (629):

> ". . . for it was after he had worshiped the Great God that he defeated the kings on the battlefield."

Thus, both allies will turn a profit: to Jarāsandha will go the *sāmrājya*, supreme kingship; to the god, as victims, the kings. Therefore, concludes Kṛṣṇa, Yudhiṣṭhira should destroy Jarāsandha for two reasons: one the personal interest in his own *rājasūya* which Jarāsandha, while he lives, makes impossible; the other, one of general morality, the deliverance of the kings who await, penned up like cattle, the time of their sacrifice.

As is frequent in the *Mahābhārata*, this revelation occasions between Yudhiṣṭhira and Kṛṣṇa a lengthy discussion, in which Bhīma gets involved. Kṛṣṇa does not conceal the fact that the expedition will be difficult: one hundred dynasties have been unable to withstand this ambitious empire-builder; the most sumptuous gifts have not averted any of his attacks. And he supplies an important piece of information (658–659):

> "What joy of life is left to the kings who are sprinkled and cleansed in the house of Paśupati [= Śiva] as sacrificial animals, bull of the Bharatas? . . . Eighty-six kings, king,

have been led to their jail by Jarāsandha; king, fourteen are left, and then he will begin his atrocity!"

And Kṛṣṇa concludes (659):

> "He who frustrated him in this would achieve a blazing fame. And he who defeats Jarāsandha will certainly become Sovereign."

Yudhiṣṭhira hesitates, Arjuna encourages him, Kṛṣṇa insists. Then Yudhiṣṭhira poses the question we are waiting for. Who is this Jarāsandha? What gives him his power, such power that he has been able to take on Kṛṣṇa himself without perishing? But before hearing Kṛṣṇa's account, let us observe that Jarāsandha fills the empty slot which remained in Śiśupāla's accordances with Starkaðr. As does the Scandinavian hero with Odin, Jarāsandha lives at least implicitly under contract to Rudra-Śiva-Paśupati. The god assures him conquests and empire, and he will sacrifice to him not one king but a hundred of them, for we are in India which is enamored of large numbers and speaks here of hecatombs, much as we have heard Kṛṣṇa promise to forgive his nephew a hundred offenses. This is how Kṛṣṇa satisfies Yudhiṣṭhira's curiosity.

2. JARĀSANDHA AND ŚIŚUPĀLA

There was an erstwhile king of Magadha, named Bṛhadratha, a great champion and warlord. He married twin sisters, the rich and beautiful daughters of the king of Kāśi, and in this double passion committed a verbal blunder (693):

> This bull among men made a compact with his wives in their presence, that he would never offend them by preferring one to the other.

Yet in vain did the king take his abundant pleasure with his two wives: he did not succeed in getting himself an heir. He went into the forest to find a hermit who, like the dervishes in oriental tales, gave him a single mango fruit, *ekam āmraphalam*, and dismissed him saying that his wish would be fulfilled (698–707). Returning to his palace, he recalled the promise he had made to the two queens, divided the fruit, gave a half to each one, and waited. The two half-fruits accomplished what he had been incapable of: to his great joy, the queens conceived. When their time had come, they gave birth—each to a live half of a boy. The poor women took counsel, and the teratological specimens were condemned. The midwives wrapped them up carefully, left by the back door, threw away their unpleasant burdens, and came hastily back inside.

A little later, a *Rākṣasī*, that is, a kind of ogress-demon, named Jarā—literally "Old Age"—who was prowling in the neighborhood, found the two half-bodies at a crossroads. It was a tempting meal. She grabbed them, and in order to carry them off more easily, joined the two halves. A marvel: they were instantly welded together, producing a well-formed and already prodigiously strong boy, who rumbled like a cloud full of rain, and would not let himself be taken away. Alerted by the commotion, the king came out with the women-folk, as well as the queens, their breasts heavy with useless milk. The demoness then reflected that, living well in the domain of this king who so ardently desired a son, she would be ungracious to eat this one up on him. She thus decided to fast this time around and, addressing Bṛhadratha, recounted the miracle to him, ascribing to herself a favorable part in it. The king forthwith declared a feast in honor of the *Rākṣasī*, and named the child *Jarāsaṃdha*, because he had been "put together, unified (*saṃdhā-*) by Jarā." Mysteriously informed of the event, the ascetic who had provided the mango came to the palace and announced the child's future. Through a shower of similes, we learn that he will have no equal in bravery, strength and power, and that all kings will obey him. Moreover, he will be invulnerable to weapons, even those hurled by gods, and above all, "transcending all the worlds with his might, the Magadhan shall with his own eyes behold Rudra, the Great God, the Destroyer of the Three Cities, he who is Hara" (748–749).

The child grows and becomes a man; his father dies and goes to heaven. He succeeds him and the hermit's prophecy comes true: nobody can withstand his conquests, and we know besides—the Calcutta text recalls it here—that, his son-in-law having been killed by the elder brother of Kṛṣṇa, his wrath is directed preferentially against that family, against the sons of Vasudeva, for whom he makes life unbearable. After this account, and with some reluctance, Yudhiṣṭhira lets himself be convinced: he must, by liquidating Jarāsandha, rescue the royal victims and make possible the *rājasūya*.

Let us pause once more to observe the great symmetry that exists between the two heroes, the king and his general, both monstrous at birth and both restored to human form at the touch of a supernatural being. Śiśupāla comes into the world with a superabundant body: two arms too many, one eye too many; if not two men in one, he is at least more than one man. In order to draw from him a human like the rest of us, one must make the third eye disappear and half of the arms drop away. Jarāsandha comes into the world in two halves, each with only half the limbs and organs of a normal human: a single eye, a single arm, and so on down to the details of his innards and the two extremities of his digestive system: a half-stomach, a half-mouth, one single buttock. To draw a normal human from him, what is needed is not pruning but welding. The magical surgery is therefore the inverse of, but has the same effect as that which Kṛṣṇa performs on Śiśupāla: in each case a monster—either by surplus or deficit—is, as Saxo says, reduced to human measure.

The miracle occurs. What is its origin, who is responsible for it? The text names Fate, *daiva*, the king's luck, *bhāgya*, of which the *Rākṣasī* has been only the means, the random agent, *hetumātra*. But behind the screen of Fate? One detail is noteworthy: it is at the meeting of four roads that the elements of the synthesis fall into the hands of the demoness who feeds on flesh and blood, and it is here, in one of Rudra's favorite domains, that the marvel occurs. Undoubtedly this is the beginning of the relationships which will unite

Rudra-Śiva and the young prince, ties more public than those which unite Rudra and Śiśupāla, who, marked at birth with the stigmata of Rudra, was transformed in a place where Rudra could not intervene: the lap of Kṛṣṇa-Viṣṇu.

Thus we have everything, in the story of Jarāsandha, that is directly useful for understanding the Indo-Scandinavian problem we are considering. But the end is interesting as it confirms that the authors have consciously established an inverted symmetry between Jarāsandha and Śiśupāla. This symmetry entails common points, between which the action develops in opposite ways.

The two common points are: the "Rudraic" character of Jarāsandha and Śiśupāla and the hostility evinced by both against Kṛṣṇa-Viṣṇu, and the decisive intervention of Kṛṣṇa in the destruction of each of them, each time after a debate over the rights of kings. But just as at their births the "pruning" of one matched the "welding" of the other, we see between these fixed points only differences and contrasts. The following list summarizes the principal ones:

1. Kṛṣṇa does not himself slay Jarāsandha, he has him killed by Bhīma, while he restrains Bhīma from killing Śiśupāla, reserving this execution for himself.

2. It is Kṛṣṇa who comes to Jarāsandha with Bhīma and Arjuna, and who provokes him and demands a duel, while Śiśupāla provokes Kṛṣṇa among the Pāṇḍavas.

3. Kṛṣṇa makes himself, in the name of royal solidarity and the morality of the kṣatriyas, the defender of kings abused by Jarāsandha, while it is Śiśupāla who, in the name of majesty and rights of kings, defends the kings allegedly offended by the homage paid to Kṛṣṇa.

4. The "Rudraic" Jarāsandha remains loyal to his god until the end, upholding and defending the cruel vow he has made to him, and after his death has no "Viṣṇuite" enlightenment, while Śiśupāla is converted in the instant that follows his death, and merges lovingly with the god who executed him.

Seen in this light, the "death of Jarāsandha" can still be of interest to the reader.[3]

3. THE END OF JARĀSANDHA

Yudhiṣṭhira's wavering has ended—an honorable hesitation, since this "Mitraic" king has been especially apprehensive of shedding the blood of others. In the end he capitulates and leaves to Kṛṣṇa the task of organizing the raid by which, he says, "Jarāsandha will be slain, the kings saved, the *rājasūya* secured" (*nihataśca jarāsandhaḥ mokṣitāśca mahīkṣitah rājasūyaśca me labdhaḥ*). Kṛṣṇa takes with him Bhīma and Arjuna, and disguised as "accomplished brahmins" ("graduates," *snātaka*), they go to the country of Magadha and arrive before its capital, Girivraja. They get in not by the door but by scaling the walls and breaking a venerated (*caitya*) monument found there, then they advance with haughty mien toward the palace. The king receives them, but he is not fooled by their disguises, and soon he shames them over their deception: what do these jewels mean on hands that show the marks of bowstrings? Why pretend to be brahmins when they radiate the elan of kṣatriyas? He calls on them to reveal themselves for what they are. With growing insolence, Kṛṣṇa answers. They are in any case authentic *snātakas*, he says, for not only brahmins, but kṣatriyas and vaiśyas too can take the vows of *snātakas*. Then he admits implicitly that they are kṣatriyas by saying that what counts among kṣatriyas is not their words but their deeds. Finally he explains their behavior: if they got into the city by the monument, it is because one gets into a friend's house by the normal entrance, and into an enemy's by a deceptive one.

Jarāsandha is surprised: he has no recollection of having been at war or having had "hostile relations" with them. Why do they regard him, innocent as he is, as an enemy? Kṛṣṇa has a ready

[3] *Mahābhārata*, pp. 67–75 (śl. 768–982).

answer. The head of a royal line has sent them, with good reason: when one keeps captive, as he does, princes from the entire world, when one has committed this cruel sin (*tad āgaḥ krūram utpādya*, 861), how can he pretend to be innocent? How does a king dare to mistreat honest kings? But (862–865, 878–879),

> ". . . having imprisoned the kings you want to sacrifice them to Rudra! The evil you have done, Bārhadrathi, might well affect us; for we follow the Law and are capable of enforcing it. Never has there been witness to human sacrifice: how then can you wish to sacrifice men to the God-Who-Appeases [Rudra-Śiva]? A baron yourself, you give fellow barons the name of beasts! . . ."
>
> "We who want to rescue the kings from you are not self-styled brahmins. I am Śauri Hṛṣīkeśa, and these champions are two Pāṇḍavas. We are challenging you, king. Stand firm and fight us, Magadhan. Either set free all the kings, or go yourself to Yama's abode!"

Jarāsandha does not lose his composure and is not without defense. Never, he says, has he sent to his dungeon a king whom he has not first vanquished; is it not the law, the *dharma* of the kṣatriya to fight, to win and then to do with the conquered whatever he pleases, *kāmataḥ*? Finally, and here is the main point, (882):

> "I have fetched these kings for the God. Should *I* now, Kṛṣṇa, let go of them, while remembering fully the life-rule of the baronage?"

His mind is made up: at the head of an army against an army, or man against man, alone against one or two or three, he is ready for battle.

He has his son Sahadeva invested as king and collects himself by calling to mind two champions who have lately contributed to his triumphs. On his side, Kṛṣṇa does not forget Brahmā's declaration: not at the hand of a member of his family must Jarāsandha perish. Therefore he will refrain. Besides, a little later, when he asks

Jarāsandha which adversary he chooses for himself, the king designates Bhīma. The court chaplain blesses his king, Kṛṣṇa blesses his champion, and there begins a spectacular duel, which lasts fourteen days. On the fourteenth day, Jarāsandha shows signs of tiring, and Kṛṣṇa urges Bhīma to let loose all his strength (929–931):

> Thus spoken to, powerful Bhīma, enemy-tamer, lifted high the mighty Jarāsandha and hurled him around; when he had hurled him a hundred times, bull of the Bharatas, he threw him down, broke his back with his knees, pounded him and bellowed forth. As Jarāsandha was being pounded and the Pāṇḍava roared, there was a tumultuous din that terrified all creatures. All the Magadhans reeled and their women aborted. . .

But Kṛṣṇa loses no time. He places his two companions in the chariot of the vanquished king, and himself goes to rescue the kings, his relatives (*āropya bhrātarau caiva mokṣayām āsa bāndhavān*) (935)—the last word indicating that the majority of the eighty-six captive kings came from the clan of the Yādavas, the object of Jarāsandha's hatred, or from allied dynasties. Freed from a terrible danger, (*mokṣitāh mahato bhayāt*), the kings shower their rescuer with gifts. Kṛṣṇa in his turn mounts the king's chariot—no ordinary conveyance, since after using it in a famous battle against the demons, Indra had given it to Vasu Uparicara,[4] and the latter in his turn had presented it to Jarāsandha's father. Seeing Kṛṣṇa leaving, the rescued kings request his orders. They receive only one: to repair to the court of Yudhiṣṭhira and attend the royal sacrifice he is about to offer. They consent—and we must thus assume that they will be part of that amorphous crowd of royalty which the erstwhile general of their former persecutor will by his demagoguery nearly succeed in turning against their rescuer.

Without doubt there is no need to keep the line rejected by the Poona edition, where Bhīma not only crushes his exhausted, dazed adversary under his knees, but also, rending him in two from head

[4] *The Destiny of a King* (1973), pp. 60–62.

to foot, restores him to the bipartite state of his birth: this must be the ingenious invention of an interpolator.[5] Whatever it is, Jarāsandha's end has more nobility than that of Śiśupāla: without madness, without intoxication, he foresees his death, consecrates his son, and fights to the end of his strength. He does not even call upon the god, in the defense of whose just offerings, as well as his cruel right to serve them up to him, he resolutely believes; moreover, every time Kṛṣṇa decides to have done with an adversary who has been protected and exploited by Rudra-Śiva, the latter, ungrateful and helpless, fails to intervene.

This story thus replicates that of Śiśupāla with notable inversions. It also completes the Indian accordances with the story of Starkaðr. How is this situation to be interpreted? The most probable explanation is that we are dealing, in India, with a literary process, an artificial duplication or reiteration. The fertile imagination of the Indian scholars has probably provided a "casting," a "miniature" replica of what the traditional story of the monster entailed "in excess," "in full"; and it probably built out this replica by reserving for it, and by amplifying, the crime which among the Scandinavians appears at the head of the three *facinora*, as the *facinus* of the first function: the king taken as victim, for a sacrifice offered to the one we have tagged the "dark god." Perhaps it is a result of this duplication that Śiśupāla has later been presented himself, in his own story, as a king among kings, remaining like Starcatherus subordinate, a "general," only in the tale of Jarāsandha.

4. APORIA

With the Indic dossier now complete, we are in a position to add a few remarks to the Indo-Scandinavian comparison which we outlined in the last chapter. Two will be inconsequential, but the last will plunge us into a quandary which the attentive reader may have noticed before.

[5] See below, p. 150.

1. The description of Jarāsandha's crime should be taken literally. Supported by the parallel Scandinavian tradition, this crime attests that human sacrifices were still practiced in earliest India. Surely the legend of Śunaḥśepa, several traditions about Manu, and the theory of the *puruṣamedha* speak in favor of its existence. But it is generally agreed that, in the form in which it is described, the *puruṣamedha* is a theoretical construct intended merely as an extension of the upper end of the sacrificial roster; and if not the wretched tale of the young Śunaḥśepa, then at least the accounts of the human sacrifices which Manu shows himself ready to perform in his obedience can also be pious inventions meant to illustrate his total absorption in *śraddhā*;[6] hence there has been interminable quibbling on the part of those who feel that it disgraces Aryan India to have had its origins in *krūra*, in cruelty. The parallelism between the sacrifices planned by Jarāsandha—even if he is, under this name, a late-comer in the story—and the sacrifice procured by Starkaðr guarantees the former the reality which the latter certainly has: Adam of Bremen still knew, by eyewitness testimony, that in Uppsala at festivals every ninth year there were hanged not only dogs and horses, but men as well, and from Tacitus' *Germania* to the *Ynglingasaga*, there are numerous attestations of human victims, offered particularly to "Mercurius" (that is, **Wōðanaz*) on the continent, and to Odin in the Swedish Uppland.

2. In the Scandinavian story, the initiative for the sacrifice in which Vikar is the victim comes from the god, Odin. He has waited patiently, through the years. Then, after he has been an undeniable help to Starkaðr in the scene of the setting of fates, and this in the presence of the beneficiary, he demands of him, as payment, that he "dispatch" his king to him. In the story of Jarāsandha the manner of agreement between the god and the man is not described, and we cannot say whether the initiative came from one or the other. But no matter; even if Jarāsandha unilaterally resolved to

[6] *Idées romaines* (1969), pp. 56–57.

promise a hundred kings to Rudra-Śiva, it was because he knew that Rudra generally pays well. There was at least a tacit understanding of the *do ut des* kind, based on the reliable taste of the god for the blood of men.

3. The victims Jarāsandha destines for Rudra are not just any men, but, like Vikar, kings. This very congruence uncovers a difficulty. In Scandinavia, all is clear: the demand expressed by Odin that King Vikar be sacrificed to him is immediately understandable since Odin, in the last analysis, only reclaims what is his, calling to himself one of his own. As the sovereign god, more precisely the king of the gods, he has an affinity, a natural intimacy with earthly kings. It is not the same in India. Rudra has no special connection with royalty, and in terms of human victims has no reason to prefer kings. One can of course suppose that he is gratified that Jarāsandha reserves for him the highest level of society, but his theological definition entails no such lofty restriction. One even gets the feeling that the specification of royal victims is forced on Jarāsandha only by the circumstances in which they are promised: since he wishes to subjugate kingdoms, he offers the actual masters of these realms to the god who can help him. This is so true that Kṛṣṇa, when he reproaches the king of Magadha for having made this bloody promise, divides his complaint into two sections, two formulae, between which the matter of royalty is deemphasized and lost in more general rules: (1) human sacrifices, he says, are criminal under any circumstances; (2) a *savarṇa* must not harm his *savarṇa*, a person of the same caste. And Kṛṣṇa does not even have in mind the possibility that the two parts of his complaint might be inseparable, and that, sacrificing men to Rudra, one should be obliged to seize kings as victims: because in reality no such obligation exists and Jarāsandha remains entirely responsible for the choice.

Nonetheless, given the close similarity of the stories of Jarāsandha and Śiśupāla, one is forced to admit that the stipulation of royalty is essential in the matter. Śiśupāla acting as passionate defender of the majesty of kings on the one hand, and Jarāsandha (whose general Śiśupāla is) capturing kings as one traps animals, to sacrifice them cruelly to a god, jointly piece together the contradictory state of affairs which is laid out more simply in the tale of Starkaðr: Starkaðr, too, is the defender of royal majesty, and yet it is against this very majesty that he commits the *facinora* to which he is doomed, beginning with the sacrificial murder of Vikar. But it is easily seen that the necessity for this situation, obvious for Starkaðr, is not so for the two Indic figures, neither for Jarāsandha nor for Śiśupāla. The reason for this lack of accordance is undoubtedly to be sought in the fact that Odin and Thor are sensed to be included in the trifunctional structure, while Rudra and Viṣṇu are outside it. The typological affinity of Rudra and Odin has been explored in the previous chapter, but Odin is no more reducible to this type than to the Varuṇa-type, and the two types which he combines in himself cannot be sundered, so that the divine pair who confront each other over Starkaðr is at once the pair of "dark god" and "light god" (in which it corresponds in fact to the pair Rudra-Viṣṇu) and the pair of first-function and second-function gods. Both at once, because, let us reiterate, in the Scandinavian theology the two pairs have been fused into one or, no doubt more precisely, because the second has been fused with the first.

In India the same is not the case. If the Vedic Viṣṇu, by the service rendered to Indra by his steps and his assistance, belongs preferentially to the second function, he spills outside it to the extent that he also serves Manu, and the sacrificer, and the gods in general; Rudra, in the hymns and later, eludes still more completely any attempt to fix him in the trifunctional structure. In Scandinavia, Viṣṇu's strict counterpart, Viðar, is very close to Thor—"the strongest of the gods after Thor"—but Viðar is homologous with Viṣṇu only in the eschatology:[7] until the end of the world, in every case, the rescuer is simply Thor, the canonical god of the second function; and the counterpart of Śiva is not so much Odin as

[7] "Le dieu scandinave Viðarr," *Revue de l'histoire des religions,* CCXVIII (1965), 1–13; *ME I,* 230–237.

one aspect of the complex Odin, and not the most important aspect, since Odin remains above all, as sovereign-magician, a figure of the first function.

If this is indeed the cause of the divergence which detains us—and no other is apparent—we find ourselves in a veritable aporia. If, setting aside the importance of kings (extolled and assassinated), we have been able to clarify the rest of the tale of Starkaðr by the related stories of Śiśupāla and Jarāsandha, it has been on condition that we retain from the pair Odin-Thor only its aspect of "dark god"–"light god," which alone allows it to be compared with the pair Rudra-Viṣṇu. But we can use the Scandinavian story to vindicate the importance of kings (exalted and persecuted) in the two Indic stories only by resorting to the other aspect of the Odin-Thor pair ("first-function"–"second-function god"), of which there is no trace in the pair Rudra-Viṣṇu.

Let us state at once that we are not in a position to reduce this difficulty, and that the third point of comparison which remains for us to consider, the story of Herakles, will rather add to it, since the two divinities we shall see confronting each other over the Greek hero are themselves defined, in this particular situation, only by their connection with the first two levels of the trifunctional structure.

But before thus extending our inquiry, we should examine a last common element in the Scandinavian and Indic stories.

V

THE WOMAN AND THE ANCESTORS

1. MASCULINE RIVALRIES

In a previous study, several examples have been given of what one might call almost a law, one of those which the authors of the *Mahābhārata* made for themselves in their work of transposing into epic a very old mythology. Composing the character and behavior of their heroes after the image of the gods whose incarnations or sons they are, they have preserved between these heroes the relationships, particularly those of hierarchy, alliance, and enmity, which existed among those gods. They have moreover sometimes translated these conceptual relationships into terms of kingship or age, transforming for example the strictly homogeneous group of gods of the three functions into the five Pāṇḍava brothers—one just sovereign, two warriors, two humble twins knowledgeable in matters of husbandry—and giving to these five brothers as their common spouse Draupadī, the heroine transposed from the single, multifaceted goddess whom the theology tended to associate with the entirety of the gods of the three functions.[1]

This blueprint which guided them, whose principle they stated but whose details they did not reveal, left them the task of supplying, of inventing human, novelistic, publishable justifications for

[1] See the discussion of Stig Wikander's discovery in *ME I*, p. 46 and n. 1; pp. 53–65, 103–109.

such predetermined relationships. For example, if Draupadī has five husbands, a scandal among the Aryans, it is, no longer from the point of view of the transposition but from that of the epic plot, the nasty consequence of an imprudent word uttered by the mother of the Pāṇḍavas. A single one of the brothers had won the girl in a *svayaṃvara* and had returned with her to the forest, to the spot where his mother and brothers awaited him. While approaching, he cried out joyously: "Here are the alms!" Before seeing him, and believing that he announced some actually divisible alms, the mother hastened to remind him of his duty: "Possess it," she said, "in common, your brothers and you." A mother's word must be done, she herself can change nothing: thus the five Pāṇḍavas had to share a single wife and give to their children a single mother; to this end they concluded a scrupulous agreement whcih they observed and which spared them any jealousy.[2]

The enmity which exists between Kṛṣṇa and Śiśupāla occasions a description of the same sort. The two figures oppose each other because one is Viṣṇu incarnate, while the other is a triply "Rudraic" being, both by the deformities which disfigure him at birth (three eyes and four arms) and by his deeply demonic nature, since he is the last of the incarnations of a demon who, at least in the preceding one, was the follower and protégé of Rudra-Śiva, and in addition by the post of general which he takes in the service of king Jarāsandha, who is also a devotee, and a cruel one, of Rudra-Śiva. Furthermore, as it always turns out when Viṣṇu confronts Rudra-Śiva or a "Rudraic" figure, the initiative in the hostilities is not taken by Kṛṣṇa, but by Śiśupāla. On all these points the transposition has respected the main lines of the theology of the two divinities.[3]

[2] Ibid., pp. 110–117.

[3] [1977] It has been objected that Śiśupāla's sixth offense against Kṛṣṇa is not homogeneous with the first five. To be sure, and perhaps I should have emphasized the difference between these treatments of the same theme: Herakles and Starcatherus perish because of the last of the three sins which they have committed and which are distributed across the three functions (likewise Indra's progressive decline is completed with and by his third, third-function sin). The fate that falls upon Śiśupāla is more complex: one after another he commits the hundred sins which, at his

But this was not enough from the standpoint of the plot, insofar as Kṛṣṇa, no less that Śiśupāla, is presented as human. Their innate opposition, glimpsed in outline, has therefore been reinforced and even overshadowed by an enmity whose cause is fortuitous and earthly, a masculine rivalry over a pretty girl. The story will be often retold in the Purāṇas, but in the *Mahābhārata* a precise allusion is made to it in the course of the very scene where we learn that Śiśupāla is on his way to exceeding, against Kṛṣṇa and his family, his credit of one hundred tolerated offenses, and that consequently Kṛṣṇa will find himself free to slay him. Kṛṣṇa himself, in a next-to-last speech, explains this strange situation to the kings to justify the beheading which is in the offing. But he ends by hurling at his prospective victim a new shot, and a cruel one:

> "For the sake of my father's sister I have endured very great suffering; but fortunately now *this* is taking place in the presence of all the kings. For you are now witnesses of the all-surpassing offense against me; learn also now the offenses he has perpetrated against me in concealment (*parokṣam*). This present offense I can no longer forbear, and his insolence amidst the full circle of kings deserves death. This fool, who must *want* to die, once proposed himself for Rukmiṇī, but the fool no more obtained her than a *śūdra* a hearing of the Veda!"

In the assembly, whose opinion is shifting back against the aggressor, the blow hits home. Here is the last retort of Śiśupāla, who knows he is doomed and shouts, with a defiant laugh:

> "Have you no shame at all, Kṛṣṇa, that you broadcast in assemblies, particularly before these kings, that your Rukmiṇī was another man's first? For what self-respecting man but you would broadcast to the strict that his wife had belonged to

---

birth, were not imposed on, but granted to, or rather tolerated of him (p. 58), and of which the five examples excerpted from the total by his accuser are well distributed across the three functions; but, by the very fact that they have been forgiven in advance, they call forth no sanctions. Consequently, in order to undo him, a supplemental sin is necessary, outside the series and extra-functional, some act of high treason directly attacking Kṛṣṇa-Viṣṇu. This enrichment of the theme does not alter its significance, but enhances it with all the mystical power inherent in the figure of Kṛṣṇa.

another, Madhusūdana? Forgive me, if you have that much faith, or don't, Kṛṣṇa, what could possibly befall me from you, however angry or friendly?"

This rivalry of two men is well known to us from elsewhere. Bhīṣmaka was king of Kundina, in the country of the Vidarbhas. He had a son, Rukmin, and a very beautiful daughter, Rukmiṇī. Kṛṣṇa loved Rukmiṇī, and Rukmiṇī loved him. Holding a grudge against Kṛṣṇa, Rukmin did not wish her to be given to him. He had him put off, then, urged on by Jarāsandha, Bhīṣmaka and Rukmin, father and son, gave Rukmiṇī to Śiśupāla. As if nothing had happened, Kṛṣṇa came to attend his rival's wedding, abducted the girl in the middle of the ceremony, and married her. Thus Rukmiṇī became what she will remain, the wife of Kṛṣṇa, of whom it is said, by the conventions of transposition, that she was the incarnation of the goddess Lakṣmī, the wife of Viṣṇu. Such is the conflict of passions which replicates the antagonism in the theological descriptions and which apparently suffices, from the human point of view, to explain the inimical relationship of Kṛṣṇa and Śiśupāla; many novels, in all literatures, are made of such stuff. One will note that each of the two men can be considered provoked by the other: Kṛṣṇa, since her parents have given to his rival the girl whom he loved and who loved him in return; Śiśupāla since, having legally and correctly received the girl, he has seen her spirited away by his rival. Without pretending to pass judgment in such a delicate affair, we will note nevertheless that in sequence, and according to the unwritten law of lovers, the first and genuinely offended one was Kṛṣṇa.

Usually the "second causes," which the authors of the *Mahābhārata* have superimposed on the deep causes arising from the translation of a mythology into epic, betray themselves as *ad hoc* inventions, often mediocre and incommensurate with what is presented as their consequence. This is the case, for example, with the rash word of the Pāṇḍavas' mother, whereby the virtuous Draupadī finds herself committed to a polyandrous marriage. One might think that it is so also for the conflict of Kṛṣṇa and Śiśupāla over

Rukmiṇī, although here the cause has the same weight as the effect, and the winning of Rukmiṇī by abduction corresponds well to Kṛṣṇa's pattern. But the comparison of the tales of Śiśupāla and Starkaðr which we are pursuing adds an important factor to the problem.

We recall how the beginning of the *Gautrekssaga*, and the texts which repeat or gloss this passage, report at the same time the birth of Starkaðr and the hostility which Thor bears him. Let us reread these important lines:[4]

> Starkaðr [Aludrengr, the first Starkaðr] was a very crafty (*hundvíss*) giant who had eight arms. From Alfheim he took Alfhildr, the daughter of King Alfr. King Alfr then called upon Thor, that Alfhildr should come back. Then Thor slew Starkaðr, and carried Alfhildr home to her father, and she was then with child. She bore a son, who was called Storvirkr, who has been mentioned; he was a man of handsome looks, although of black hair, bigger and stronger than other men. . . .

To this Storvirkr and his legitimate wife, the daughter of an earl of Halogaland, was born the second Starkaðr, the hero of the saga.

We recall also that in a later episode, the saga has something more, and perhaps different, to say: a clear allusion is made to a masculine—one dare not say romantic—rivalry between the monstrous giant and Thor. At the moment when Thor and Odin, in the assembly of the solemnly gathered gods, contradictorily determine the fate of the second Starkaðr, Thor declares himself from the beginning against the boy, and reveals his grievances:[5]

> Then Thor began to speak and said: "Alfhildr, the mother of Starkaðr's father, chose as father to her son a very crafty giant rather than Thor of the Æsir, and I declare this for Starkaðr, that he shall have neither son nor daughter, and so shall his line end."

[4] Above, p. 12.
[5] Above, p. 14.

Is the schematic account of the beginning of the *Gautrekssaga* incomplete? Do the two passages refer to two variants, one where Thor intervened, disinterestedly, only at the request of Alfhildr's father, the other where he avenged himself on a successful rival? In any case this second text exists, and describes a situation similar to, and partially the converse of, the one which opposes Śiśupāla and Kṛṣṇa over Rukmiṇī: first, the giant and the god both desire the girl; second, the giant takes her, with her consent; third, the god kills the giant, retakes the girl and returns her to her father; but fourth, the god remains offended that the other had been preferred to him to the point of begetting in his place. The revenge he chooses is well suited to the nature of this resentment: he punishes the guilty ones through their grandson, whom he condemns to have no progeny, to be the last of his race. Thus in Scandinavia as in India a second cause overlies the deep cause, independent of logic and self-sufficient: it is the generalized, unexceptioned hostility of Thor against all that comes from giants. The god's attitude toward the hero is justified by a novelistic incident, a variation on a theme which literatures never tire of presenting to a no less indefatigable public: two men and a woman. In both cases, in Scandinavia and in India, the god ends by slaying his rival; only in the saga the rival is not the hero of the story but his grandfather, and the killing follows on the heels of the offense; in the *Mahābhārata*, Kṛṣṇa's rival is Śiśupāla himself and the killing is long postponed (but note that at least it follows immediately the reminder which Kṛṣṇa gives of their rivalry). In both cases, the god "recovers" the girl; only in the Scandinavian tale it is for her father and not for himself, and the girl is pregnant; in the *Mahābhārata* it is during the wedding ceremony, before Rukmiṇī has really fallen into Śiśupāla's power, that Kṛṣṇa gets hold of her, still virgin, and marries her. This last disparity is moreover only the natural consequence of another, more important one: it is the giant, the first Starkaðr, whom Alfhildr has chosen, spurning the god Thor, while it is the incarnate god Kṛṣṇa whom Rukmiṇī prefers to the "Rudraic" and demonical Śiśupāla.

One should therefore hesitate to discard the novelistic prelude of the saga—as I have lately done myself[6]—for the a priori reason that "woman trouble" is alien to Thor's character. It may be on the contrary that, in this piece of literature, the god who is normally above human weaknesses—love, desire, jealousy—shows himself by virtue of a very ancient tradition singularly unequal to himself.

2. REINCARNATED DEMON AND GRANDSON OF A GIANT

This consideration constrains us not to reject summarily the other strange feature of the saga version: the duality of Starkaðr, a grandfather and a grandson. To be sure, it could be easily imagined that a *sagamaðr*, bothered by a tradition which insisted on the birth in the form of a giant and monster of a hero whose life, apart from three incidents, is and should be edifying, has split up the character, relegating the repugnant elements to a first Starkaðr and reserving for a second one, his entirely human grandson, the reasons the reader has for admiring him. However, things may have gone the other way; Saxo may have simplified an initially more complex situation. And here again it is the saga's version which reinforces, against Saxo, the comparison with the Indic account.

The hostility which exists between Kṛṣṇa and Śiśupāla is not hereditary: Kṛṣṇa has had no quarrel with the father, nor with a grandfather, of the little monster. But, as we have seen, neither is it without precedent. The Indian notion of reincarnation simply replaces heredity and gives it a cosmic dimension: Śiśupāla is but the latest form taken by the demon who was, in the last "crises" in which Viṣṇu had to intervene, Hiraṇyakaśipu and Rāvaṇa—figures who, like Jarāsandha, long enjoyed the protection of Rudra-Śiva, but who in the end, like Jarāsandha, and occasionally for having made themselves intolerable to Rudra-Śiva himself, found themselves abandoned by their protector. Let us quote once again

[6] *The Destiny of the Warrior* (1970), p. 93.

Colonel de Polier, in the pages which open his résumé of the *Rāmāyaṇa,* or rather the account of it which his Indian tutor, Ramtchound, is supposed to give him. Thus on Rāvaṇa:[7]

> "Raven was ruler of the isle of Lanca, or Ceylon. Like all the ambitious Daints [demons], he aspired to the conquest of Paradise, and to succeed in this he had devoted one hundred years of his long life to worshipping Mhadaio [Mahādeva, Rudra-Śiva] and had obtained from this Deiotas, by sacrificing his head to him, not only the normal recompense of ten more heads and as many arms, but also the privilege of being unable to be put to death unless there should be cut from him a million heads."
>
> "But he had only ten of them," said M. de Polier.
>
> "He had only ten at a time," replied the teacher, "but they would regrow to the extent that they were cut off, the which rendered his defeat so difficult that there was no one but Viṣṇu who could destroy him. Not content with the extraordinary gifts he had received from Mhadaio, he coerced Birmah, by threatening to kill him, to bestow on him a net and a javelin, miraculous weapons which the terror-stricken Birmah granted him although he foresaw the evil use which he would make of these gifts, in addition to which this giant had also such prodigious strength that, wishing one day to awaken Mhadaio from one of his trances, he transported with one hand this Deiotas and his residence onto the summit of Mount Hermantchel, the abode of the father of Parbutty [Parvatī, the wife of Rudra-Śiva].
>
> Drunk with his power, his strength and the privileges Mhadaio had granted him, the pride and ambition of the Daints grew proportionately, and he no longer dreamt of anything but making himself master of the whole universe. He had already subdued the earth and Paradise, he had encroached upon hell, and by his tyranny he became the object of such universal terror and hatred that Birmah and Mhadaio themselves, alarmed at the abuse he had made of the supernatural

[7] Cf. above, p. 81, n. 4. This passage in I, 292–294.

and miraculous gifts they had given him, awaited with as much impatience as the lesser Deiotas the moment when the foretold incarnation of Viṣṇu would come to pass. The impiety and the crimes of Raven at last fill the term fixed by the decrees of fate as the time for his punishment, and everything heralds the great event which must bring to an end the reign of vice, restore virtue on earth and make manifest the exclusive power of Viṣṇu."

It is this Rāvaṇa who, slain by Viṣṇu in the guise of Rāma, will be reincarnated as Śiśupāla and so will for the last time confront Viṣṇu, who has become Kṛṣṇa.

It is doubtful, in spite of Celtic evidence, whether one should trace back to Indo-European times the belief in metempsychosis, in successive reincarnations. In any case it is alien to the Germanic world. But continuity in family lines, functionally speaking, plays the same role. It has long been noted that one of the name-giving patterns observed in certain periods by the Scandinavians, as well as by numerous other peoples, was to name newborn children after close ancestors:[8] no doubt they thought in this way to be doing a little more than reviving a memory or an image; even rationalized to the extreme, such a practice at least charts for the newborn a life-plan, an imitation which, if adopted and carried out by the namesake, in the last analysis reanimates the deceased himself. Is it not this belief that has been able to justify the coexistence of Starkaðr, father of Storvirkr, and Starkaðr, son of Storvirkr, and at the same time, the two interventions of Thor, killing the one and persecuting the other? This diachronic timing of happenings, this prenatal stage at least gives the hero's life story a scope comparable with, although less cosmic than, that conferred on Śiśupāla by his demonic past and his prior encounters in other lives with the same god.

These last comparisons to be sure leave with no ready answer the problem of the relative value of the two versions of the birth of Starkaðr. If they restore between them the balance of chance,

[8] *Mythes et dieux des Germains*, pp. 61–62; K. A. Eckhardt, *Irdische Unsterblichkeit, germanischer Glaube an die Wiederverkörperung in der Sippe* (1937).

which until now has leaned to the side of Saxo at the expense of the saga, they do not allow us to decide. Is it necessary to prefer one or the other, Saxo or the saga? Or must we suppose that each one continues what were already, from earliest times, "variants"? For the first of the two themes we have been examining—the resentment of a god against the son of a woman who has preferred a rival to him—the legend of Herakles will, however, recommend a decision against Saxo, in favor of the *sagamaðr*. But, in the Greek legend, the genders of the deities are reversed in relation to their roles: it is a goddess, Hera, who persecutes the son whom her less than faithful spouse, Zeus, has chosen to obtain through the services of her involuntary rival Alkmene, the wife of Amphitryon.

VI

HERAKLES

1. THE FAILINGS OF HERAKLES

In 1956 I gave reasons, which still seem valid, to consider the life of Herakles, like that of Starkaðr-Starcatherus, not as the huge and fortuitous accretion of specific legends, independent and self-sufficient, each tied to a town, province, lake, or forest, the exploits of a strongman, but more as a structure whose general design is simple and which has only served as a framework—wealth attracting wealth—for a variety of legends, local or otherwise, concerning the Strong Man.[1]

This general framework is that of the "three sins of the hero," and I have recalled at the outset of this study what these sins are, each one committed against the principle of one of the three Indo-European functions:[2] since my *Aspects de la fonction guerrière* the dossier has not changed. Herakles performs his feats in three groups, each ending with the "functional sin" and the corresponding penalty or consequence, which affect first the hero's sanity, next his bodily health, and finally his life. Moreover the penalties are not cumulative, and the first two cease to operate once sufficient expiation has been effected. The intervals filled with exploits

[1] *The Destiny of the Warrior* [1970], pp. 96–97. For the systematization of the *Library* of Apollodorus (II, 4,8–7,7), see ibid. p. 102 n. 6.

[2] Cf. above, pp. 1–6.

are distributed thus: the first runs from the hero's birth to his hesitation before the command of Zeus, with madness as penalty;[3] the second extends from his insubordination to the treacherous murder of a surprised enemy, with physical disease as its penalty; the third goes from this murder to his scandalous adultery, with the consequence of an unhealable burn and his voluntary death. Within the first of these three groups appears, as a sub-group, the collection of ten or twelve great Labors, which has itself served to lodge sub-labors, and which is the only partial structure that can be discerned within the large framework. As for the sins, the biography of Herakles presents more than one deed which we would be inclined, even in Greek terms, to classify as such, but the fact is that only these three have been fastened on by the gods and had a destructive effect on the guilty party.

The parallel with the three sins of Starcatherus is accompanied by other accordances in the careers of the two heroes. The main ones were pointed out in 1956, but the investigation of Śiśupāla reveals their full importance. They concern, on the one hand, the hero's birth and his resulting position in the trifunctional structure, especially the contrary relationships which it establishes between him and two rival divinities; and on the other hand his death.

2. HERA, ATHENA AND HERAKLES

The birth of Herakles is recounted by Diodorus Siculus (IV, 9, 2–3) after recalling that on both sides the hero "owes his birth to the

[3] [1982] Several writers who have referred to the book seem to have understood the first fault of Herakles to be the killing of his children in his madness. This is not quite right: his *failing* is having disobeyed the command of Zeus by hesitating to go into Eurystheus' service, and thus compromising the agreement reached between Zeus and Hera regarding a matter of kingship; the *punishment* consisted in a madness whose result, calling for *expiation*, was the murder of his children.

greatest of the gods": Zeus is his father, and his mother Alkmene descends from Perseus, the son of Zeus and Danae:

> 2. . . . The prowess which was found in him was not only to be seen in his deeds, but was also recognized even before his birth. For when Zeus lay with Alkmene he made the night three times its normal length (τριπλασίαν τὴν νύκτα ποιῆσαι) and by the magnitude of the time expended on the procreation (τῷ πλήθει τοῦ πρὸς τὴν παιδοποιίαν ἀναλωθέντος χρόνου) he presaged the exceptional might of the child which would be begotten (προσημῆναι τὴν ὑπερβολὴν τῆς τοῦ γεννηθησομένου ῥώμης).
>
> 3. And, in general, he did not effect this union from the desire of love, as he did in the case of other women, but rather only for the sake of procreation (τῆς παιδοποιίας χάριν). Consequently, desiring to give legality to his embraces, he did not choose to offer violence to Alkmene, and yet he could not hope to persuade her because of her chastity (σωφροσύνη); and so, deciding to use deception, he deceived Alkmene by assuming in every respect the shape of Amphitryon.

Herakles is thus neither monster nor giant—even if speculations on his more than human size have not been lacking—but, like Starcatherus, he has in him a certain excess, ὑπερβολή, a surplus of strength in relation to other men, resulting from a watered-down form of triplicity: Zeus spent three nights begetting him, thus allowing for this single insemination an amount of sperm which seems, even for a god, to have been considerable.

The position of Herakles in relation to the first and second functions, and particularly in relation to the two goddesses who preside over them (Diodorus, IV, 9, 4–8):

> 4. When the natural time of pregnancy had passed, Zeus, whose mind was fixed on the birth of Herakles, announced in advance in the presence of all the gods that it was his intention to make the child who should be born that day king (ποιῆσαι βασιλέα) over the decendants of Perseus; whereupon Hera, who was filled with jealousy (ζηλοτυποῦσαν), using as her

helper Eileithyia her daughter, checked the birth-pains of Alkmene and brought Eurystheus forth to the light before his full time.

5. Zeus, however, though he had been outgeneralled, wished both to fulfill his promise and to take thought for the future fame (ἐπιφανεία) of Herakles; consequently, they say, he persuaded Hera to agree that Eurystheus should be king as he had promised, but that Herakles should serve Eurystheus and perform twelve labors, these to be whatever Eurystheus should prescribe, and that after he had done so he should receive the gift of immortality (βασιλέα μὲν ὑπάρξαι κατὰ τὴν ἰδίαν ὑπόσχεσιν Εὐρυσθέα, τὸν δ' Ἡρακλέα τεταγμένον ὑπὸ τὸν Εὐρυσθέα τελέσαι δώδεκα ἄθλους οὓς ἂν ὁ Εὐρυσθεὺς προστάξῃ, καὶ τοῦτο πράξαντα τυχεῖν τῆς ἀθανασίας).

6. After Alkmene had brought forth the babe, fearful of Hera's jealousy (ζηλοτυπίαν) she exposed it at a place which to this time is called after him the Field of Herakles. Now at this very time Athena, approaching the spot in the company of Hera (καθ' ὃν δὴ χρόνον 'Αθηνᾶ μετὰ τῆς Ἥρας προσιοῦσα) and being amazed at the natural vigor of the child (θαυμάσασα τοῦ παιδίου τὴν φύσιν), persuaded Hera to offer it the breast (συνέπεισε τὴν Ἥραν τὴν θηλὴν ὑποσχεῖν). But when the boy tugged upon her breast with greater violence than would be expected at his age, Hera was unable to endure the pain and cast the babe from her (ἡ μὲν Ἥρα διαλγήσασα τὸ βρέφος ἔρριψεν), whereupon Athena took it to its mother and urged her to rear it ('Αθηνᾶ δὲ κομίσασα αὐτὸ πρὸς τὴν μητέρα τρέφειν παρεκελεύσατο).

7. And anyone may well be surprised at the unexpected turn of the affair (τὸ τῆς περιπετείας παράδοξον); for the mother whose duty it was to love (στέργειν ὀφείλουσα) her own offspring was trying to destroy it while she who cherished towards it a stepmother's hatred, in ignorance saved the life of one who was her natural enemy (δι' ἄγνοιαν ἔσωζε τὸ τῇ φύσει πολέμιον).

Various forms are taken, especially during Herakles' youth, by the enmity of Hera and the solicitude of Athena. If we stick with the text of Diodorus, it is Hera who sends the two serpents which the infant strangles in his cradle, thus, it was claimed, winning his heroic name: "He who owes his glory (κλέος) to Hera" (10, 1); it is Hera too who strikes him with madness because he hesitates too long to enter the service of Eurystheus (11, 1). Where various gods arm and equip Herakles, it is Athena who presents the first gift, a *peplos* (14, 3). Later, according to the *Library* of Apollodorus, it is to her, no doubt as his most trusted friend, that Herakles hands over the apples of the Hesperides, which the goddess immediately returns to their place (II, 5, 11).

The two goddesses clearly have here the contrasting values attributed to them also in the legend of the judgment of Paris:[4] Hera is the sovereign, whose first concern is to exclude Alkmene's son from royalty and to reduce him—this is the gist of the compromise she accepts—to the role of champion, obedient to the king. Athena immediately takes the future hero under her protection, rescues him when he is only an abandoned baby, sees to his outfitting, and follows him discreetly in his labors. The two goddesses, to be sure, do not combat each other, they even walk together, but their harmony is only outward. This is no longer the alliance into which they were driven, in the legend of the shepherd prince Paris, by their common enmity toward Aphrodite; they play antagonistic roles, and the virgin Athena does not hesitate to trick Hera, to get her to nurse with her own milk the child whom the fearful Alkmene had exposed in the countryside. This scene of the goddess saving and nursing the child whom she will thereafter persecute, and who begins by biting her, recalls, functionally speaking, the initially ambiguous relationship of Śiśupāla and Kṛṣṇa: placed on the god's knees, the little monster receives human form, he is saved; but at the same time the plan of a long hostility is laid.

As for the attitude of the hero himself toward the two higher functions—the kingship from which he has been excluded, and the "labors," that is, essentially, fights, to which he has been con-

[4] *ME I*, pp. 580–586.

signed—it is more dramatic than that of Starkaðr-Starcatherus, who, born far from any throne, confines himself (outside of his three sins, directed against them) to serving kings ostentatiously; and more pathetic too than Śiśupāla's, a king who voluntarily becomes the general of another king. Herakles' first sin is precisely to hesitate, despite the command of Zeus, despite the warning of Delphi, to become the champion of King Eurystheus: he judges him and knows himself to be superior to him. But after his first punishment he submits, seeks and receives the king's orders, προστάγματα, left to enjoy now and then the bitter satisfaction he gets from the spectacle of his mediocre master: vase paintings have popularized the scene where he brings back to the king the wild boar of Erymanthus; he carries the boar alive on his shoulders; panic-stricken, the king hides in a barrel (φοβηθεὶς ἔκρυψεν ἑαυτὸν εἰς χαλκοῦν πίθον; Diodorus, IV, 12, 2). But never, either during or after the long term of the labors, does he raise a hand against the king, nor attempt to replace him; and never, throughout the journeys where he redresses so many wrongs and punishes so many evil men, does he propose to become king himself: he lends, and if need be, imposes his services, sometimes gets a reward for them, then takes his leave.

3. THE END OF HERAKLES; HERAKLES AND HERA

The Death of Herakles, Hera reconciled (Diodorus, IV, 38, 3–5; 39, 2–3):

After his adultery, Herakles is trapped in the cloak dipped in the blood of Nessos. Informed of her husband's passion for Iole, Deianeira recalled the present the dying Centaur had given her. Had he not told her that, if her husband came to neglect her, to rekindle his passion she need only have him put on a cloth rubbed in his blood? What she did not know was that in the Centaur's blood lingered the poison of the arrow which which Herakles had pierced him. Thus she sent, saturated with what she thought was a love potion, the sacrificial cloak that Herakles had asked for. He put it on, and activated by his body's heat, the poison began to devour him. In the grip of the growing, intolerable pain, the hero sent two of his companions to consult for a third time the oracle of Delphi, and Apollo responded, "Let Herakles be taken up to Mount Oeta in all his warrior gear, and let a pyre be erected next to him; for the rest, Zeus will provide."

> 4. Now when Iolaüs had carried out these orders and had withdrawn to a distance to see what would take place, Herakles, having abandoned hope for himself, ascended the pyre and asked each one who came up to him to put torch to the pyre. And when no one had the courage to obey him Philoktetes alone was prevailed upon; and he, having received in return for his compliance the gift of the bow and arrows of Herakles, lighted the pyre. And immediately lightning also fell from the heavens and the pyre was wholly consumed.
>
> 5. After this, when the companions of Iolaüs came to gather up the bones of Herakles and found not a single bone anywhere, they assumed that, in accordance with the words of the oracle, he had passed from among men into the company of the gods.

After a few remarks on the establishment of the first cults of Herakles (39, 1), Diodorus makes us partake of the secrets of Olympus:

> 2. We should add to what has been said about Herakles, that after his apotheosis Zeus persuaded Hera to adopt him as her son (υἱοποιήσασθαι) and henceforth for all time to cherish him with a mother's love, and this adoption, they say, took place in the following manner. Hera lay upon a bed, and drawing Herakles close to her body then let him fall through her garments to the ground, imitating in this way the actual birth. . . .
>
> 3. Hera, the myths relate, after she had adopted Herakles in this fashion, joined him in marriage to Hebe, regarding whom the poet speaks in the "Nekyia":

Herakles meets up with Geras (Old Age), one of the many guises in which death dogged him throughout his heroic career (compare the premature *senex* Starcatherus, in spite of his three lives).

I saw the shade of Herakles, but for
Himself he takes delight of feasts among
The immortal gods and for his wife he has
The shapely-ankled Hebe.[5]

4. HERAKLES, STARKAÐR, AND ŚIŚUPĀLA

There are immediately perceptible analogies with the end of Starcatherus, and others with the end of Śiśupāla, with the peculiarly Greek addition of the important theme of the pyre and the apotheosis.

Like the Scandinavian hero, the Greek one determines to die, seeks a killer, and finds him in the person of an innocent warrior, who acts, to be sure, out of devotion, but whose service he rewards: Starcatherus returns to Hatherus the blood price he had received for killing his father and offers as well to ensure his invulnerability, by a means which the latter finds suspect and does not use; Herakles hands over to Philoktetes arrows to whose great and fearsome power the future, and Sophocles, will testify: they alone will make possible victory over the Trojans, but first one of them will poison its possessor and cause the Greeks to abandon him, alone, on an island.

As with the Indian Śiśupāla, his death completely reconciles the hero with the divinity who has been, by his own fault in India, in spite of him in Greece, his enemy. India goes so far as to have the very being of Śiśupāla absorbed into the divinity; the more rational Greece speaks of a contract which transforms enmity into adoption and filiation, with a scenario simulating not a fusion but a birth, and which is futhermore completed immediately by the wedding to Hebe, daughter of the inimical goddess, in the sort of union which is at once most intimate and least miraculous, namely marriage.

It seems impossible to attribute to chance so many similarities which appear on both sides in the same order. But this affirmation

[5] [1982] On Deianeira and the marriages of Herakles in general, see my *Mariages indo-européens* (Paris: Payot, 1979), pp. 59–63.

marks the limit of our grasp. The divinities who confront each other over Herakles under the fairly passive supervision of Zeus, his protectress and his persecutor, intervene, as in the legend of the shepherd Paris, strictly as patrons of the first two functions: the Sovereign who withholds from Herakles the expected kingship and subordinates him to a king, and the Warrioress who in his person foresees, loves and favors the courageous victor of labors and fights. No feature sets them in opposition in the guise of what we have termed, in connection with the other two heroes, the "dark divinity" and the "light divinity."

Thus we find ourselves faced with a paradoxical situation, with Scandinavia able to provide only a typologically middle term, and not a geographically intermediate one. We leave the reader before this aporia, which will perhaps lead other minds to a more subtle analysis of one or more of the divine pairs, but which for the present does not allow comparison of the Greek and Indic pairs:

GREECE	SCANDINAVIA	INDIA
Hera, 1st function	Odin { 1st function	
	Odin { "dark divinity"	Rudra, "dark divinity"
Athena, 2nd function	Thor { 2nd function	
	Thor { "light divinity"	Kṛṣṇa-Viṣṇu, "light divinity"

The comparativist can only entrust to Hellenists, those who control the vast literary, archeological, and philosophical mass of data on Herakles, the task not only of resolving this aporia but of making use of the accordances it provides them. It seems that Herakles, well before being torn in his will, courtesy of Prodikos, between the attractions of vice and virtue, had found himself the passive and impotent pawn in another rivalry, this one from the beginning already in his Indo-European prototype. This rivalry of divine powers secured for him a happy end, but at first, from deed to misdeed and misdeed to deed, made him roam throughout the islands and peninsulas of the Mediterranean, while by similar fate his "lost brothers" traversed other climes, one the vast lands stretching from the Bosporus to the fjords of Norway, the other the mosaic of the realms of India. Perhaps, though, we will be allowed a comment, if not a suggestion. Does not the parable of Prodikos confer on the conflict which Herakles is embroiled in something of the value, entirely moral and not at all functional, which opposes the implicit Rudra and the explicit Kṛṣṇa-Viṣṇu with respect to Śiśupāla? Perhaps this parable, which Marcel Détienne has already managed to push back in time,[6] continues an interpretation of the pathetic son of Alkmene which is even older than the Pythagorean Herakles and the antecedents that can be postulated for him. Perhaps Hera and Athena, *interpretationes Graecae* of the Indo-European divinities of the pre-Heraclean story, have diluted the more complex type, closer to the Scandinavian version, of these divinities, and the elements thus lost have run aground, or flourished, under the philosophical rubrics of Good and Evil, Vice and Virtue.[7]

[6] "Héraclès, héros pythagoricien," *Revue de l'histoire des religions*, 158 (1960), 21–53, with extensive bibliography.

[7] [1982] Neither in this chapter, nor in *The Destiny of the Warrior* which it summarizes, have I maintained that *all* of Herakles, with his complex character, his adventures, his posthumous hero-god status, and his cults, fits into the framework of the "three functional sins of the warrior"; Herakles is neither Starkaðr nor Śiśupāla, and each of these heroes has his own personality. I wished only to make it probable that this framework, although attested as such, in full, only in the summaries of Diodorus and the *Library*, was ancient and Indo-European, and that the Heraklean material, vast and open-ended, found it ready to be assimilated and integrated. Indeed I foresaw that there would be Greek specialists who would accuse me of an imperialism which I do not practice. It was even a pleasant surprise for me to have so long to wait (*Aspects de la fonction guerrière*, the first version of *The Destiny of the Warrior*, dates from 1956). Finally, after 25 years, my wait is over. In the article "Héraclès" which Nicole Loraux compiled for the *Dictionnaire des mythologies* (Flammarion, 1981), one reads (1: 497b) that "Herakles cannot be reduced either to the Dorian hero of Wilamowitz, or to the vegetation daimon dear to

J. Harrison, or to the Dumézilian warrior with his three sins." Where did I make this distressing "reduction"? Although several passages in her article suggest that she would be of some help, no one requires Loraux to associate herself with comparative studies for which she clearly has no taste, but since she feels obliged to pronounce sentence, should she not keep up with current developments? In 1981 she was still familiar only with *The Destiny of the Warrior* ("the book as a whole sheds more light on the figure of Herakles than the pages explicitly devoted to his three sins, which, by attempting to prove too much, are not very convincing"), and she was unaware of *Mythe et épopée II*—including the present work—with the confirmations and mediations, as well as new problems, added to the dossier by the legend of Śiśupāla.

Summary

In the three works we have compared, what might be called the isothemes, or boundaries among congruences and divergences, are not all drawn in the same way.

The largest bundle of isothemes joins on one side Greece and Scandinavia, against India on the other.

1. The divinities who oppose one another on the subject of Herakles and Starkaðr are those of the first and second functions, while Kṛṣṇa-Viṣṇu and Rudra-Śiva do not fit into the trifunctional structure and are comparable with Odin and Thor only in other aspects.

2. The divinity with whom Herakles is reconciled after his death is Hera, the wife of the sovereign Zeus; the one who lurks behind Hatherus and who benefits (or could do so) from Śiśupāla's last gift is Höðr, very close to Odin, the god at once sovereign and "dark" (in the sense we have given this term). On the other hand Śiśupāla, at the instant of his death, is reconciled with the "light" divinity, Kṛṣṇa-Viṣṇu, and merges with him.

3. Herakles and Starkaðr are sympathetic heroes, the first having no "demonic" component, the second having lost along with his monstrousness whatever "gigantic" elements resulted from his birth. Śiśupāla, on the other hand, until the conversion that takes place at the moment of his death, remains the being, at once demonic and Śivaistic, which he has been from birth.

4. Neither Herakles nor Starkaðr has provoked the divinity who persecutes him: they suffer his enmity, the cause of which

antedates their birth. Śiśupāla on the contrary never ceases until the end to try the patience of Kṛṣṇa-Viṣṇu, who in fact does not persecute him, but finally punishes him.

5. However important the activity of the divinities who are in conflict over Herakles and Starkaðr, still it is the hero himself who is interesting, and once past the beginnings the deities fade into the background, though they are felt to be present and watchful. It is Kṛṣṇa-Viṣṇu on the contrary who is the main character, Śiśupāla being only an episodic figure, a sort of incorrigible Indian Loki, in the only thing that is really important, the career of the incarnate god.

6. Consequently the reader comes out on the side of neither Odin nor Thor, but of Starkaðr; he is certainly not for Hera, rather for Athena, but above all for Herakles himself, and for Athena only to the extent that she helps him. In contrast, from one end of the story to the other we are for and with Kṛṣṇa-Viṣṇu.

7. In particular, the voluntary deaths of Herakles and Starkaðr are good and serene, despite the ordeals which cause them—the decrepitude of age and his remorse from his third crime for Starkaðr, and the insufferable burning which results from his third crime for Herakles. Śiśupāla's death is on the contrary the climax of a frenzied delirium.

8. Only the stories of Herakles and Starkaðr introduce the figure of the young man whom the hero entreats to liberate him from life—a noble act, to be sure, but one which is nonetheless remunerated.

9. In these two cases alone, the offer or final gift is ambiguous: Hatherus is suspicious, and we will never know if he had reason to be; the poisoned arrows given by Herakles will wound Philoktetes incurably.[1]

10. The general type of Herakles and Starkaðr is the same: redresser of wrongs, wandering hero, given to toil, πόνος.

11. Consequently each is an educator: in Saxo, the episode of Frotho's children restored to virtue by Starcatherus has no other

[1] [1977] On the variants of Philoctetes' wound, see P. Vidal-Naquet, "Philoctète et l'éphébie," *Annales E.S.C.* 26 (1971), 625 (Sophocles) and 630 (Servius, *ad Aen.* 3.402).

meaning, and Herakles is known to have a role in the upbringing, as well as protection, of young Greeks.

12. Starkaðr has a reputation as a great *skald*, the foremost of the *skalds*; tradition attributes to him poems on his own deeds and the mythic battle of Bråvalla, and, in the saga as in Saxo, the "gift of poetry" has been conferred on him by Odin. The association of the Muses and Herakles (μουσικὸς ἀνήρ, *Hercules Musarum*; and already on sixth-century vases Ἡρακλῆς κιθαρῳδός, Herakles the pupil of Linos) is ancient, undoubtedly older than the iconographic attestations and the Pythagorean speculations.

But other accordances bring together India and Scandinavia in contrast to Greece, and sometimes spectacularly so. Thus:

1. Śiśupāla and Starkaðr are born with monstrosities which are corrected, before their careers begin, by one of the two divinities concerned. Herakles has no birth defects.

2. India and Scandinavia place importance on royal ideology, stressing the attitudes of the two heroes toward kingship and providing emphatic statements on the subject. The Greek legend outlines the theme in the beginning (the opposition of Eurystheus and Herakles) but does not dwell on it.

3. The faults of Śiśupāla and Starkaðr are foreordained: imposed on the one at birth by his demonic nature and ancestry, on the other by the "lots" annunciated, according to the variants, by either Odin or Thor. Herakles commits his three crimes freely.

4. Taking into account that the legend of Jarāsandha completes that of Śiśupāla, India and Scandinavia charge their heroes, implying criminality, with one or more human sacrifices, the sacrifice of one or more kings offered or promised to the "dark" divinity who demands them. Nothing like this occurs in the long career of Herakles.

5. The manner of death is the same for Starkaðr and Śiśupāla: each has himself beheaded, one with composure and on his own request, the other in a giddiness of aggression. Herakles mounts a pyre.

6. Starkaðr, like Śiśupāla, has to do with only two opposing divinities (*Höðr being functionally indistinguishable from Odin),

with no higher judge: This is natural and unavoidable in Scandinavia, where Odin is the highest, sovereign god; in India one might have expected, overarching the opposition of Rudra-Śiva and Viṣṇu, some intervention, some "plan" of Brahmā, but there is none. On the contrary, above Hera and Athena who vie for Herakles, there is Zeus, whose paternal concern, though frustrated, nonetheless carries the day. This complication of the pattern, made possible in Greece by the fact that the functional divinities are here goddesses (as in the parallel case of the legend of the shepherd Paris), adds to the interest and pathos of the life of Herakles.

Finally, other correspondences draw together India and Greece, and separate them from Scandinavia.

1. Formally, the three functional failings of Śiśupāla and Herakles are close in kind. The third is one of sexual libido for each of them, while for Starkaðr it is *auri sacra fames*. The second failure consists of an unworthy betrayal of a warrior both in the case of Herakles, who surprises and throws down Iphitos instead of fighting him, and in that of Śiśupāla, who twice profits from a king's absence to harass his town or his officers, whereas for Starkaðr it consists of a shameful flight on the battlefield. The first failing offends a god in the case of Herakles who resists the command of Zeus, and a sacrificer in the case of Śiśupāla, who by stealing the horse planned as an offering by a king, strikes a blow at an act of worship, whereas in Starkaðr's case it results from an excess of obligingness towards a god (it is true that on this point the legend of Jarāsandha, complementary to that of Śiśupāla, juxtaposes conversely Scandinavia and India).

2. In consequence of this first difference, Śiśupāla and Herakles (in the latter case even though Aphrodite does not intervene as such in a career dedicated to Hera and Athena alone) have no enmity, quite the contrary, against the third function in its sensuous aspect, while Starkaðr, whose entire destiny is fixed by Odin and Thor, condemns this kind of weakness, and in Saxo makes clear his contempt and distaste for "Fro," the Freyr of Uppsala, and his "effeminate" festivals.

This varying distribution of similarities and differences, let us note in passing, is a powerful argument in favor of the hypothesis of a common inheritance from an Indo-European original. The fact that the Scandinavian form of the tale is, in many respects, intermediate between the Greek and Indic forms, should be borne in mind.

Comparison of the three tales helps in defining the position of the three heroes in the varying theological frameworks in which they are included.

As for Scandinavia, it is now clear that I was mistaken, in 1956, in trying to understand Starkaðr (or rather Starcatherus, as the evidence was all drawn from Saxo) as a "hero of Thor," contrastable with the well-known Odinic heroes, Sigurðr, Helgi, and the others. It is elsewhere, in the *Gesta Danorum*, in Book VII, as has been well shown by Paul Herrmann,[2] that a "hero of Thor" is to be found, in the person of Haldanus Biargrammus. Starkaðr himself is an Odinic hero, but of a rare type (in fact he is the only example), linked to the dark aspects of this complex god. The nobility of Sigurðr is spotless, while Odin from the beginning makes Starkaðr his accomplice. Handsome, brilliant, young, well-loved, winning his fame in his natural environment, until his tragic death Sigurðr heaps up exploits, not "labors," while Starkaðr, abnormally laden with years and disfigured by huge and innumerable wounds, solitary and forbidding, wanders across the world, in pain and suffering like Herakles.

Regarding Greece, Herakles certainly continues to appear, in terms of this study, as what he seems to be, a second-function hero, on the order of the Vedic Indra and even more, no doubt, on the order of the other Indo-Iranian patron of the warrior function, Vāyu, and his epic transformation Bhīma. But the Scandinavian parallel compels us to pay more attention to his touching relationship with Zeus, and at the same time to emphasize the originality of Greece. A second drama, in the world of the gods, duplicates the hero's trying career. Zeus, his father, desires the happiness of a son with

[2] *Kommentar*, pp. 479–481.

whose begetting he has taken especial pains, and yet causes at first, if not his unhappiness, at least his πόνος, in a long series of physical and moral trials. Zeus, king of the gods, destines him to a splendid kingship among men, but is forced to compel him into the service of a grotesque king. Zeus, master of the fates, is made to feel in this most important case the limits of his mastery, the risk that lies in setting his decrees into formulae: the formula turns against his intention, against his protégé. And since every sequence of tragedies must end with some less weighty drama, the final apotheosis of Herakles is also the end—for the time being—of another dispute, the eternal conjugal strife of inconstant Zeus and his ill-resigned spouse.

The Indian Śiśupāla, at least in the form in which we know his legend, is more difficult to place. The overriding fact is his complete changeover from good to evil, or rather the total elimination of the good elements which formed the essence of his prototype where the sins, the three sins, were only a glaring exception. But, thanks to the consolatory philosophy of Viṣṇu, the thinkers and artists of India have made of this very debasement the stuff of a sublime "mystery": the excess of hatred transformed at the moment of death into the fullness of love; an individual demonic life losing itself, with no expiatory stage, in the ocean of the divine life.

As for the three functional sins of Indra in the *Mārkaṇḍeya-Purāṇa*, it now seems likely that they have to do with a secondary realization, an artificial extension to mythology, of the epic theme of the "three sins of the warrior," detached from the structure of which it formed a part since Indo-European times, and whence the tale of Śiśupāla is derived directly.

Have other Indo-European peoples besides the Indians, Scandinavians, and Greeks preserved, by transforming it in other ways, the epic structure we have been considering? Up to the present, after quite a few soundings, the answer remains negative. Given the conservatism of the Romans and the mythical origin of the accounts from which they compiled their oldest history, one might expect to find among them a variant attached to the third king, Tullus Hostilius, who characteristically represents the second function, *rei militaris institutor*, as his predecessors Romulus and Numa do the first function, one founding his whole career on the divine *signa*, the other establishing *sacra* and *leges*. But no: Tullus to be sure is in trouble with Jupiter, who ends by blasting him, and he carries many a victory, but Mars does not intervene in his life. It is all the gods, collectively, whom he scorns and neglects, and Mars does not contend with Jupiter for him, nor favor him against Jupiter. As for the numerous great warriors of the Irish legends, none is the subject of a tale which, nearly or remotely, recalls those which we have been studying.[3]

In the story of Starkaðr-Starcatherus and in that of Śiśupāla, as we have stressed, the ambiguous relationship of the hero and royalty is obvious, giving rise not only to deeds, but to theoretical discourses on the majesty of kings. This similarity between the Germanics and the Indians is noteworthy. Added to it is another, mentioned in the first volume of *Mythe et epopée*, in connection with the god Heimdallr and Bhīṣma, the heroic transposition in the *Mahābhārata*[4] of the sky-god Dyauḥ.

Heimdallr, like Bhīṣma, is a "framing figure," in the sense that he is the "first" and "last" in time: in mythical time in the case of Heimdallr, who is born before and dies after all the gods; in "historical" time in that of Bhīṣma, who belongs to an earlier generation

[3] [1982] This statement has been brilliantly contradicted by David J. Cohen, *Celtica* 12 (1977), 112–124. In the *Buile Suibhne*, the life of the errant warrior Suibhne Geilt is punctuated by two actual failings and one false accusation which leads to his death: he offends St. Ronan; he flees from the battlefield of Magh Rath; accused of adultery, he dies a violent death in the house of St. Moling, but not before receiving the last rites from the saint's hands.

The gathering of attestations of this theme goes on. Daniel Dubuisson has found an inportant one in the structure of the second Indian epic: see "Trois thèses sur le Rāmāyaṇa," *Annales E.S.C.* 34 (1979), 464–489 ("the three failings," pp. 466–474; "from three failings to three functions," pp. 474–477). Other versions, in other Indo-European societies, are presently being analyzed.

[4] *ME I*, pp. 182–190.

than the protagonists of the *Mahābhārata,* but who thanks to a special privilege lives through as many generations as he wishes and dies after them in the great transposed eschatological battle—at least after those of them (all the "good" ones save the five Pāṇḍavas, and all the "evil" ones) who must die there. Both of them, too, maintain the same kind of relationship with royalty. Bhīṣma, by his right of seniority, ought to be king: he renounces this right and makes himself the guardian of the dynasty, marrying off the princes and assuring the coming of each generation into the world, then the education of the king and his brothers. Heimdallr, notwithstanding his temporal priority, is not the king of the gods, which title belongs to Odin. But, in human form and under the name of *Rígr* ("king," not in Germanic, but in Irish), he ensures successively through three generations the birth of the ancestors of the three social Estates (slaves, peasants, noble warriors), and from the children of the latter—ancestors of the *jarlar*—he selects a boy to whom he gives individual tutoring, passes on particularly a magical knowledge, and confers the name of *Kon-ungr* ("king" in Old Icelandic, but not in Irish), and who becomes indeed the prototype of kings.

We see that in these two cases, in the tales of the "first" hero and the "second-function hero," the Scandinavians and the Indians bring in royalty in order to describe its relation to what, being closest to it, could but does not enter into conflict with it: Heimdallr and Bhīṣma avail themselves of their priority only to "prepare" kings; Starcatherus and Śiśupāla theorize about and extol royal power, and, save for the sins imposed on them by fate or their nature, respect and defend it among, before, and if need be against kings. In other words, in both cases it is lateral aspects of kingship which are considered: not its workings, but its connections either with what precedes it mythically—Heaven before the sovereign gods, Janus before Jupiter, etc.—or with what actually follows it in the social order—or, as Tacitus says, the *dux* next to the *rex.*

Let us avoid premature conclusions: the comparative exploitation of legends has only begun. But let us note that the Indo-Germanic isothemes seem to mark off another domain than that accompanying the Indo-Celto-Italic isolexeme of the name of the king (Skt. *rāj-*, Celt. *rīg-*, Lat. *rēg-*): whether in institutions or in other kinds of epic tales (one of which is the subject of a separate treatment)[5] it is the workings, the chances, and the internal or external risks of kingship which make for comparison among the "*rēg-societies."

In any case it is certainly not by chance that, on the one hand, the didactic section of the tale of Starkaðr (assuredly old, and confirmed by *Beowulf*), that is, the scene where Starcatherus by his exhortations transforms the mock king Ingellus into a real king, has acquired a length which seems at first inordinate; nor that, on the other hand, the story of Śiśupāla, with its complement, the story of Jarāsandha, has been used by the authors of the *Mahābhārata* on the occasion of the *rājasūya*, or royal consecration, of Yudhiṣṭhira, these two heroes constituting the two obstacles to this consecration, one as rival, the other as objector. Perhaps it is even thanks to its connection with royal rituals that this material in both instances has been preserved since prehistory.

Our final comment will be to emphasize that a new example of "Indo-European literature," specifically Indo-European epic literature, has come to be added to an already well-stocked file: it is impossible to believe that the three tales we have considered were composed independently, starting simply from the same preserved Indo-European "ideology," and that their continued similarity is the result of secondary convergence.

It is above all the Scandinavian tradition which has made this result possible, reminding us that this same tradition, compared with those of several other Indo-European peoples, and especially

[5] *The Destiny of a King* (1973).

the Indic branch, has enabled us to glimpse a number of ancient epic-mythical tales. We now know of a "world drama" (the death of Baldr and Ragnarök and the central plot of the *Mahābhārata*),[6] as well as the "history" of the formation of a whole society by the war and subsequent reconciliation of the representatives of the first two functions with those of the third (Æsir and Vanir; Proto-Romans and Sabines; *devas* and Aśvins),[7] with the latter extending to the creation and dismemberment of the monster Drunkenness (Kvasir, Mada).[8] And among other more properly epic stories, there is the one whose existence Stig Wikander established by juxtaposing the antecedents, circumstances, and episodes of the Scandinavian battle of Brávellir (Bråvalla) with a series of precise and important features in the Indic battle of Kurukṣetra, features of which the central plot of the Mahābhārata gives no account.[9]

[6] *ME I*, pp. 208–240.

[7] *Archaic Roman Religion* (1970), pp. 66–73; *ME I*, pp. 288–290.

[8] *Loki* (Paris, 1948), pp. 97–106 (German edition [1959], pp. 67–74).

[9] See "Från Bråvalla till Kurukshetra," *Arkiv för Nordisk Filologi* 74 (1960), 183–193: cf. *ME I*, pp. 255–257.

Appendix

Excerpts from the "Mythology of the Hindus" by the Canoness de Polier

In the interest of rescuing from oblivion the "Mythology of the Hindus,"[1] I reproduce the pages containing the description of the deaths of Jarāsandha[2] and of Śiśupāla.[3] No doubt the reader will prefer to see for himself the changes the legends have undergone in this first presentation of the *Mahābhārata* in a Western language.

1. JARĀSANDHA

[Yudhiṣṭhira has just informed Kṛṣṇa that he intends to celebrate a *rājasūya* and that he needs his help to fulfil the difficult conditions of this undertaking.]

"What then," asked Mr. de Polier, "is this Raisoo-yuc [= *rāja-sūya*]?"

"This ceremony," answered the teacher [Ramtchund, Polier's instructor], "also called the festival of the Rajahs, could be celebrated only by a ruler who had vanquished and subdued all the

[1] Above, p. 81, n. 4.
[2] I, 603–614; cf. above, pp. 97–107.
[3] I, 614–619; cf. above, chap. II.

other sovereigns of the world. It was necessary for all the Rajahs of the universe, willingly or by force, to be gathered together at the residence of the one who held the Raisoo-yuc. And this ceremony had so many requirements that Judister [Yudhiṣṭhira], although he had been reestablished in power, could never have brought it to pass without the aid of Chrisnen [Kṛṣṇa]. But although the son of Basdaio [Vasudeva], by reading these letters of his protégés, already knew what he had to do, he still wished to appear to take counsel. Thus, calling upon Oudho [Uddhava], he asked him for his advice. 'Since the Pandos [Pāṇḍavas],' he told him, 'have begun the preparations for the Raisoo-yuc only in the belief that I would help them, and since it is time for the Rajahs held in chains, who have claimed my protection, to be delivered, do you think, Oudho, that by yielding to the wish of my cousins these two objects might be achieved?'

Oudho, animated by a prophetic spirit, knew the intentions of the head of the Yadus [Yādavas]. Thus he answered, 'The difficulties to be encountered in the celebration of the Raisoo-yuc cannot have escaped the insight of so wise a prince as Judister; he has certainly realized that by his forces alone he could not subdue the Rajahs of the four quarters of the universe. Nevertheless he is preparing his ceremony in the firm belief that with your powerful aid his undertaking will have a happy outcome. Therefore, O Chrisnen, I advise you to accede to his invitation, the more so because, as the time has come to rescue the captives who groan under the chains of Jerashind [Jarāsandha], the yuc [*yajña* 'sacrifice'] announced by Judister will be the occasion of his punishment because, too proud to accept the invitation of the head of the Pandos, it will be necessary to force him into it, and whatever trust he has hitherto placed in his strength, which surpasses that of ten thousand elephants, and in his invulnerability, I foresee nevertheless that Bhim [Bhīma], the second of the Pandos, his equal in every respect, supported by you, will inevitably defeat him, and thus the two objectives which concern you will be achieved.'"

"But why," asked Mr. de Polier, "had Chrisnen spared Jerashind until then? Could he not have taken his life as he had so many others?"

"Of course he could," answered the teacher, "but Chrisnen, as a divine being, knew the decrees of fate; he knew the date set for Jerashind's death, and that he could be killed only by Bhim and at a time when he, Chrisnen, was present; this is why not only did he not kill him himself, but he even prevented Bulhader [Baladeva, or Balarāma, Kṛṣṇa's brother] from killing him. And Oudho, inspired as he was, who also knew these facts, could predict the outcome with certainty. Be that as it may, all the Yadus applauded the advice that he gave to Basdaio's son. And so the latter ordered preparations to be made immediately, and on the following day made his departure with great pomp and magnificence, accompanied by the noblest chiefs of his tribe and a large corps of troops, and followed by a multitude of elephants and camels carrying the baggage, and a number of chariots laden with thrones, crowns and all sorts of arms. Messengers preceded Chrisnen, charged with announcing to the Rajahs held captive by Jerashind that he was coming to their aid. Crossing in this way the modern kingdom of Soorethe [Surāṣṭra], he came upon the borders of Meevat [Meerath?], where he found the Rajah Judister advancing to meet him, accompanied by Munis, Brahmins, and choirs of instrumental and vocal music, who preceded a large and brilliant procession. Although the son of Basdaio, being younger than Judister, always insisted on tendering him the respect due his age, this Rajah hastened to anticipate him, and falling down at his feet, he sprinkled his hands with the tears of joy that he was made to shed by the favor that the Avatar [Kṛṣṇa, the incarnation of Viṣṇu] had granted him. Chrisnen raised him and embraced him, and gave a most kindly welcome to his four other cousins, and then, finishing with the amenities which he customarily showed to the Rishis, Munis and Brahmins, he went on with them to Aindraprest [Indraprastha] or Delhi, the capital of Judister's country. . . .

A few days after Chrisnen's arrival, the head of the Pandos convened an assembly of the four castes, attended by the most celebrated Brahmins. Addressing himself to Chrisnen, who was presiding, he told him 'that by his arrival in Aindraprest, he felt himself already raised to the heavens and capable of any undertaking; that in daring to conceive the grand design of celebrating the Raisoo-yuc, he had relied on the constant affection which the son of Basdaio had always deigned to bestow upon the Pandos; that, although he knew that in the eyes of the creator of the universe all men were equal in worth, yet he believed that those who, feeling the need which they had for divine assistance, requested it with faith and humility, would have the good fortune of obtaining it.' Judister's words seemed to please the Avatar. He assured him that his trust would not be disappointed and that the creator of the universe would accord him his protection. 'I see,' he added, 'that you have already prepared the things necessary for the sacrifice, but at present it is necessary to see about assembling here the monarchs and warriors of the four corners of the world, and it is for your four brothers, whose valor sets them above all the Deiotas [*devatās*, divinities], to bring them to Aindraprest. Therefore let Bhim go to the west, Arjoon [Arjuna] to the north, Schecdaio [Sahadeva] to the south, and Nakul [Nakula] to the east. As for you, Judister, awaiting their return, put all in readiness to begin your yuc.'

The victories of the four Pandos being as rapid as was their travel, they soon returned, followed by all the rulers whom they had defeated, and bringing with them an enormous booty and wealth. But Jerashind had withstood them, he alone could not be subdued. Judister, dismayed and seeing in this the ruination of his whole plan, made known to Chrisnen all the anguish which the thought produced in him. Oudho, who was present at the conversation of the two cousins, began to speak. 'I have always been of the opinion,' said he, 'that Jerashind cannot be conquered as other Rajahs. To draw him into a single combat one must use strategy. Thus, let Chrisnen, Bhim and Arjoon call upon him in the guise of Zennadars [astrologers]. He has no equal in generosity: open-handedness, he says, is the primary duty of a ruler; all perishes in this world, but the name of a free-spending man will live forever.'"

"He could afford to be," interrupted Mr. de Polier, "since he had expropriated the wealth of 20,800 Rajas."

"Also," the teacher went on, "Oudho assured them that this renown lay so close to his heart that, by introducing themselves to him as poor Brahmins, they would be sure not only of being admitted, but of obtaining everything they might ask of him.

Chrisnen approved of Oudho's advice, and the three cousins, in the dress of Zennadars, betook themselves to Mogah [Magadha]. They were introduced to the Rajah, who knew as soon as he saw them, by their speech and by the distinguishing marks of Kättris [*kṣatriyas*], that these three strangers were no Brahmins. Despite this he welcomed them as such, and said to them, 'O Brahmins, what do you wish of me? Whatever you ask of me, from the smallest gift to that of a kingdom, you shall not leave here without obtaining it, and though I am convinced that you are no Zennadars, this thought will have no more influence upon me than the arguments of Soucker [Śukra] upon Baly [Bali]. So speak fearlessly!' Chrisnen then stepped forward and requested a samgram [*saṃgrāma*], or single combat, adding 'Since you know that we are not Brahmins, learn too that here is Bhim, the second of the Pandos, Arjoon his brother, and I their cousin.' At these words Jerashind turned to his courtiers and smiled contemptuously, exclaiming, 'I admire the insolence of this churl, whom I have often put to flight, and who, too happy to save his life, still dares to provoke me into another battle. Very well, I accept, I grant a samgram. You have escaped my hand only by abandoning Mathra [the town of Mathurā], and saving yourself in the sea, but where will you hide now? And yet,' he added, 'it is too loathsome for me to do battle with a mortal whom I have already defeated; Arjoon is too young and delicate, no doubt he does not pretend to the honor of fighting with me; Bhim, who is stronger, is the only one of you worthy of attempting it, if he has the courage. Let him be given other clothing, and choose arms which he can use.' Bhim chose a club, Jerashind had one brought to him, and the two champions, followed by Chrisnen and Arjoon, went to the battleground, surrounded by the Rajah's troops and a multitude of onlookers.

Before beginning, Jerashind addressed to himself the Nemeskar [*namaskāra*], or reverence, that is due God, then he kissed his own hand. Thereupon he advanced against Bhim, and the event began, their clubs striking each other with such violence that the vault of heaven reverberated with the sound they made. The clubs were soon broken to splinters, and they had to take recourse to spears, to swords, and to axes. With all these arms reduced to pieces, the two combatants resorted to fisticuffs, again with such an even skill that one might have thought they had had the same master in the art of fighting. After battling in this way for the entire day without the least advantage on either side, in the evening the three cousins and Jerashind ate together and slept under the same roof. Twenty-seven days had already passed in this manner, when Bhim gave a signal to Chrisnen that he believed he was exposed to too much danger, for this fight was beginning to exceed his strength and his ribs were broken and bruised from the blows he was receiving, while he, Chrisnen, a mere spectator, had not taken the least hurt. He added that as for himself, were it not for the shame of admitting he was beaten, he would gladly give up this battle. Arjoon, understanding the silent words of his brother, became pale with fright, but Chrisnen, replying to Bhim by signs even more expressive than his own, reproached him for his discouragement and lack of faith just when success was in his grasp. Then, getting up and plucking a blade of grass, he took it by the stem and tore it from bottom to top, showing Bhim how on the next day he should split the body of his adversary. Bhim, understanding his divine protector, suddenly felt his strength renewed. Filled with a new vigor, on beginning the battle the next day, he threw Jerashind to the ground, and before he could recover, took one of his legs in each hand and split his body to the top of his head, as Chrisnen had torn the blade of grass."

"But how was it that Jerashind, until then so equal in strength, all of a sudden became so inferior?" asked Mr. de Polier.

"According to the explanations of the Brahmins," replied the teacher, "Jerashind, knowing his horoscope, knew the only way in which he could be slain. He understood that Chrisnen's sign had indicated it to Bhim. This knowledge made his blood freeze in his veins, weakening him to the point of a man in his last moments. Thus all the credit for his defeat rests solely with the divine Avatar. But as it was Bhim who was the instrument which he used, in the eyes of mortals it was he who received the honor of the victory. Chrisnen and Arjoon applauded, the Deiotas threw flowers at him, while the people and the army, astounded at the death of their sovereign whom they had believed invincible, stood motionless. The son of Basdaio lost no time in crowning Jerashind's son king, and ordered him to release his father's captives. Then, accompanied by the new Rajah of Mogah and this brilliant entourage, he took once again the road to Aindraprest where all the Brahmins and the Rajahs of the world were gathered. The lords of the Coros [Kurus, Kauravas], Dirtratch [Dhṛtarāṣṭra], Biskum [Bhīṣma], and Durdjohn [Duryodhana] himself had come there; Birmah, Mhadaio [Brahma, Mahādeva or Śiva], all the celestial hierarchies with their heads, the birds and animals of every species were gathered there. For save for the two Raisoo-yuc celebrated by King Ainder [Indra], the lord of heaven, and by King Bären [Varuṇa], the lord of the seas, no one had ever seen the like of that which Judister was about to celebrate. All mankind was in astonishment and admiration at the profusion of gold and riches used in the ornaments, the vessels and the raiments for the sacrifice, but a few sages, seeing Chrisnen presiding over this festival, understood the reason why it surpassed those which had been seen before."

2. ŚIŚUPĀLA

"With everything ready, and the various offices to be fulfilled during the ceremonies assigned, the rite began with a sacrifice;

Judister, dressed in a splendid tunic, placing a golden cord in the hands of the Zennadars, holding in his own the Cusa [*kuśa*] or sacred grass, advances toward the altar, offers the oblation, and while pronouncing the name of Narreye [Nārāyaṇa], which means spirit or divine breath, his glances turn toward Chrisnen, with the smile expressing the gratitude which, attributing all the success of his undertaking to the presence of his divine protector, also regards him as the primary object of his love and his offering; with this preliminary act accomplished, before commencing the individual pujas [non-sanguinary offerings], Judister addresses the heads of his family, asking them to decide the important question of who, in this august ceremony, should have the honor of the first of these sacrifices? No one answers, then Schecdaio, the fourth of the Pandos, arises and observes in a modest and respectful tone that in asking this question his elder brother already knows its answer, for, he goes on, 'there can be no doubt in this respect, and since Chrisnen is in this assembly, the first puja should be addressed to him, as the Veds [Vedas] say expressly that an oblation presented to him has the same virtue as a sacrifice offered to all the Deiotas, just as in watering the root of a tree one gives life to the smallest of its leaves.' Chrisnen, the speaker continued, 'is the creator, the preserver, the destroyer of the universe, in his oneness he is all, the earth and all the creatures are the body of which he alone is the soul and the spirit. As for me,' Schecdaio added, 'I shall always worship only him.' Full of his subject, he was about to continue his discourse, but Chrisnen restrained him. Nevertheless, the majority of the assembly applauded what he had just said, and Judister, satisfied of the decision which he had wished for, washed the feet of Chrisnen and poured this same water over his head and his eyes, after which, setting before him the splendid raiments, gems, precious chains and all the paraphernalia of the puja, he set about the beginning of it by prostrating himself at the feet of his divine protector. But while the lord of the Pandos was busy with these holy offices, the Deiotas intoned the hymns to Bhagavat, and the pious men said their prayers, a loud murmur arose in the asembly, several prideful Rajahs grumbling at the preeminence accorded to the son of Basdaio. More incensed than the rest, Souspal [Śiśupāla], Rajah of Chanderi, stood out because of his anger. He had never forgotten the abduction of Roukmani [Rukmiṇī] and his shameful defeat, and his only wish was to avenge himself. The resentment which he harbored made this new triumph of his rival insufferable to him. Rising from his place, with rage in his heart and fury in his eyes, he interrupted the celebration of the puja: 'How,' he cried out arrogantly, 'how can the Brahmins tolerate such abuse? What then are the titles, the station, the nobility of Chrisnen that he merits this preeminence in such an august assembly, filled with the noblest individuals, the most learned Zennadars, the lowest of whom is more qualified than he? Do you not know,' he continued, 'that the Yadus are accursed, that they shall never wear the diadem, that no noble rank can be accorded to that contemptible creature who deserted Mathra to seek a refuge in the middle of the sea, to establish there a den of bandits scattered and fled from all corners of the earth, at whose head he claims to launch a new religion?'

The audacity with which Souspal disturbed the majestic ceremony, and the outrageous claims he showered upon Chrisnen, began to agitate the spectators. But Basdaio's son stilled them by his signals and prevented them from interrupting his enemy. Yet his insolence grew to the point where several members of the assembly, unable to suffer it any longer and finding it indecent, unworthy of themselves, and even criminal to listen to his blasphemy, left the enclosure where he was speaking, while Bhim and his brothers looked for their weapons in order to punish Souspal, who for his part was getting ready to fight. Thus everything foreboded a scene of confusion and horror which by interrupting the sacrifice would have prevented the celebration of the Raisoo-yuc itself. But Chrisnen, now intervening more directly, forbade the Pandos all physical recourse, ordering them to prevent all that might precipitate it, and addressing Souspal, told him that, in view of the circumstances, he would tolerate from him one hundred more insults, with the warning that when this number was exhausted he would punish him himself. This magnanimity of Basdaio's son, far from stopping the prideful Rajah, incited him all the more, and he quickly exceeded the prescribed limit. Then Chrisnen, giving free reign to his righteousness, threw at him his ring Sudarsun [Sudarśana, the discus of Viṣṇu], which at one stroke cut off his head, from which issued a flame which seemed for a few moments to hover in the air, after which it entered at last into the mouth of the Avatar, while the servants and troups of Souspal fled in the greatest disorder."

"Tell me then, teacher, what was this flame?" asked Mr. de Polier.

"It was," answered the teacher, "the soul of the Rajah. Dying directly at the hand of the Avatar, it received his grace and was freed from reincarnations to return to Baikunt [Vaikuṇṭha, Viṣṇu's paradise] and take the place it had held as the doorkeeper of Viṣṇu."

"Then Souspal," replied Mr. de Polier, "was one of the manifestations of those doorkeepers condemned by the curse of the Rishis to be reincarnated three times on earth?"

"Precisely,"said the teacher. "We have seen them reincarnated in the bodies of Herncashup [Hiraṇyakaśipu] and Hernachus [Hiraṇyākṣa], two Daints [*daityas*, demons] who were brothers, who occasioned two avatars or incarnations of Viṣṇu, one as a wild boar and the other as a man-lion. Their second incarnation was in the bodies of Raven [Rāvaṇa] and Kuntchbeckaren [Kumbhakarṇa]; that necessitated the incarnation of Ramtchund [Rāma]. And finally, in the third, they fought against the incarnation of Viṣṇu [as Kṛṣṇa] and were freed by him from the bodies of Souspal and his brother Denthebek, in which they finished the term of their transmigrations."